No Stable Too Small

Fifteen Christmas Plays For Churches Of All Sizes

Lois Anne DeLong
and
Barbara Anne Antonucci

CSS Publishing Company, Inc., Lima, Ohio

NO STABLE TOO SMALL

For more information about CSS Publishing Company resources, visit our website at www.csspub.com or email us at custserv@csspub.com or call (800) 241-4056.

Cover design by Barbara Spencer
ISBN-13: 978-0-7880-2408-5
ISBN-10: 0-7880-2408-6
PRINTED IN U.S.A.

I'd like to dedicate this volume to all the children at the Brentwood Presbyterian Church who first spoke these lines, to the young people of GSG Productions (Godsongs Group) whose talent, energy, and natural creativity continue to inspire my growth as a playwright, and to the young people of "Creaciones" in El Salvador who have taught me that theatre can change the world. The book is also dedicated to my family — mother Elizabeth, sister Ruth, nieces Aimee, Kristina, Melissa, and Stephanie, and great-niece Samantha — for not only never questioning my excursions behind the curtain, but for often taking the trip with me. Lastly, I thank the giver of all good things for the precious gift of words, and for the opportunity to do what I love most — spark young imaginations through theatre.

— Lois Anne DeLong

These plays are dedicated to all the "Baby Angels" that have passed under our wings, including my daughter, Robyn, the Baby Jesus who never made it to the manger, and my son, Michael, who grew to play multiple roles as required, often all in the same show! Also to my husband, Pat, who stood by us through the crazy writing, rehearsals, and Christmas Eves spent wrangling those "Baby Angels."

I would also like to thank Reverend James Watson, who suggested Lois and I work on a Christmas program so many years ago. I guess you knew, Jim, "If We Do It, It Will Work"!

— Barbara Anne Antonucci

Table Of Contents

Birthing A New Kind
Of Christmas Pageant

No Stable Too Small is a work 25 years in the making, and we are both delighted to be able to share these plays that have been so special to us with pastors, Christian education directors, Sunday school and pre-school teachers, and anyone else who picks up this volume. While we feel the works speak for themselves, a little background on how they came to be might provide the answer to the question, "Do we really need another collection of Christmas plays?"

If you had found yourself in the position we were in back in 1979, you might be quick to say, "Yes." When we were put in charge of doing a production for the annual Christmas Eve family service, we checked the plays in many of those other collections, and found nothing to suit our purposes. All the scripts we saw were:

Too long: As a component of a family-friendly worship service, we needed something that would run no longer than twenty minutes.

Too elaborate: Calling for full sets, authentic costumes, and numerous props.

Too full of characters: Featuring casts way too large for our available "child pool."

Too dated: With characters talking in a stilted, saccharine way that no self-respecting Generation-Y child ever would.

At the time, we were both members of a small church with a small Sunday school. Our church had no budget for sets, costumes, or props. We wanted to do productions that spoke to the children we were working with, so they would actually look forward to taking part in the play. We also were interested in finding fresh perspectives from which we could hear the message of Christ's birth.

We wanted our plays to teach the children the full context of the Christmas story, including the prophecy which Christ's birth fulfilled. And, we knew we wanted something deeper, more meaningful, and frankly, funnier than the average pageant. Laughter is one of God's great gifts, and satire can be a very effective way of getting a point across.

Since we both had a theatrical background, the answer was obvious. We would write and stage our own original productions that would allow us to:

- expand or contract the number of roles based on the number of children with which we had to work any given Christmas;
- offer fresh interpretations of the story of Christ's birth that affirmed for children their role in spreading the good news of the gospel; and
- could be produced without sets and with minimal props and costumes.

We would stuff these plays with biblical facts *and* intentional anachronisms, such as having the Angel Gabriel refer to baseball in one play, an angel pass out sunglasses in another play, and setting a very contemporary talk show in the ancient world in yet another. The results can be found in this volume.

These plays have been tested and tried by some pretty tough critics — a generation-plus of four- to fourteen-year-olds. Through these plays, many of the children not only connected on a deeper level with the true message of Christmas, but also developed a lifelong love of theater. In 1999, we launched Godsongs Youth Theatre, a program designed to give young people a voice to speak their dreams, fears, frustrations, and joys through the medium of theater. To date, this group has produced seven (soon to be eight) original full-length plays with music. All but one member of that original cast had their start in our Christmas plays, and all could recite some of the basic theater mantras they learned from this experience, such as "You have nice butts, but we don't want to see them" (said to keep them from turning their backs to the audience!).

We offer these plays to our fellow small churches, and hope you might find in them what you might have been looking for in planning your Christmas programs. If your church or organization is blessed with additional people and resources, we still feel you'll find this book of value. The plays are designed to be expanded or contracted as needed by reassigning lines, so you can accommodate larger casts. And, there's nothing that says you *can't* use sets or better costumes if you have the means to construct them. As the years went by, we actually began incorporating some additional theatrical elements, such as lighting effects. All we ask is that you keep in mind the message of one of the plays in this book, titled "It Wasn't The Hilton, You Know." Our Savior was born in the humblest of settings. God knew that simple is often better.

We also invite you to adapt these plays to fit your unique group of children, and to keep them fresh. If any references feel outdated, change them. If you have more children than roles, write in new characters. A play is a living, breathing piece of writing and, as such, should never be completely "done."

Here's to many Merry Christmases.

Lois Anne DeLong
Bay Shore, New York

Barbara Anne Antonucci
Monroe, North Carolina

Some Tips For Using These Plays

Categories

When we were organizing and sequencing these plays, we needed some way to decide what should go where. There were a number of ways we could have done this, but we decided it might be best to break them into Basic, Intermediate, and Advanced Plays. The criteria for this division were a bit fuzzy. "Basic" plays could be characterized as such if they were short in length, featured small casts, had very simple themes, and speaking parts that could be mastered by younger children. "Intermediate" plays were those that worked with mixed age ranges, but still leaned toward the simplicity needed for younger children. "Advanced" plays were deemed those best done by older youth that dealt with more sophisticated themes. But, in some ways, these labels were very arbitrary. If you're new to staging Christmas plays, don't automatically avoid the Advanced Plays, as you might have just the right cast available to perform it. Similarly, don't automatically write-off the Basic Plays as being too simple for your group. By layering on some theatrical effects, and elaborating on some of the roles, it could contain just the message your church needs.

Staging

The staging included in the plays is from their original productions at the Brentwood Presbyterian Church. The plays were presented in the church sanctuary, which features a raised platform, two side transepts, doors to hallways on the right and left aisles, and a choir loft at the back of the sanctuary. We also have a room at the end of the sanctuary area, making it easy for actors to enter from the back of the space. All the staging is very simple and can easily be re-worked for any space. For those new to the theater, "stage right" and "stage left" always refer to the actors' right and left on stage; "downstage" is the front portion of the stage, and "upstage" is the back portion.

11

Casting

We have found that the number of girls volunteering for the plays will usually outnumber the boys. This could be problematic, since male characters in the Christmas story clearly outnumber the females. Our answer to this problem is, except for the parts of Mary and Joseph, to simply ignore gender barriers. This is one reason why most of our characters do not have names, and are just referred to as Child 1 or Angel 3. We have presented plays with girl shepherds and girl kings (and, no, we don't then call them "We Three Queens.") We have also had boys play angels by writing the (presumably male) characters of Gabriel and Michael into several scripts. Any act of theater requires a leap of faith on the audience's part, a "suspension of disbelief," as it is called. Casting girls in male parts may reduce their historical accuracy, but does not in any way dilute the impact of the play's message.

Costumes And Props

True to our goal of writing plays that any church can produce, even those that can't afford sets or costumes, all the plays that appear in this volume can be staged with what we call "representative costumes." This means using just one or two costuming elements to tip the audience off as to who the character is supposed to be. For shepherds, this usually meant tying a scarf (or at times, a dish towel) around their heads. For the kings, we've found that a belted choir robe makes a great kingly robe. For the "sheep" used in one play, we dressed the children in white shirts, and made headpieces with ears out of foam. And, we found, for the little ones, you can make a perfectly good angel costume by cutting a neck and two armholes out of a white pillowcase. Tinsel garlands make great halos, but angels don't need wings. The pride on their faces as they say their lines can be as radiant as any wings.

In terms of props, we mostly wrote in common items that we could take from our own houses, or make out of "found" materials. A passable scroll can be constructed from paper towel rolls and construction paper, and logs for a fire can be made from rolled up newspapers.

We encourage you to think along the same lines with your productions. Chances are you have at least one person in your church that is skilled at making something out of nothing. We encourage you to invite him/her/them to be part of your team, and see what they can do. Let them have a go at it. God inspires. Wait and see what he can do. He inspired us.

Music

We often enhanced our productions by playing music at the beginning and end of plays, or in-between scenes. We encourage you to look beyond the traditional Christmas hymns. Pop songs can often add that unexpected edge that makes the message that much more accessible.

Curtain up!

The best piece of advice we can give in staging these plays is to be prepared for anything. Have back-up costumes, and if possible, back-up children or youth you can pull on stage at the last minute, if need be. If not, be prepared to think on your feet. Several times we've been blessed to have a "live Baby Jesus," a baby from the congregation whose parents let us place him or her onstage in a manger for a few minutes during the play. It can be a beautiful addition to a production, but it's not without its complications. One year, our Baby Jesus was unable to attend due to an ear infection. Lacking a proper understudy, we wrapped up a stuffed Snoopy for the manger. (That Baby Jesus has made up for her absence in the manger that year. She has appeared in numerous Christmas plays as she was growing up, and has been an active member of our Godsongs Youth Theatre program since 1999.)

But for every production where children froze on stage, or wandered off their marks, or started crying because someone took the halo they wanted, there were wonderful moments of improvisation where everything just came together. It's those moments that make staging these plays worth the trouble.

Basic Plays

*Spare, short, simple plays
for small casts and young casts*

Love Finds A Way

Characters (in order of appearance)

Singer 1	Joseph Mohr
Singer 2	Franz Gruber/Guitar Player
Singer 3	Austrian Choir Member 1
Singer 4	Austrian Choir Member 2
Singer 5	Austrian Choir Member 3
Assistant Choir Director	Austrian Choir Member 4
Choir Director	

Props

Choir robes
Wool scarves
Sheet music — English and German versions of "Silent Night"
Guitar

Notes

"Love Finds A Way," which tells the story behind the writing of "Silent Night," requires a relatively small cast of mixed ages. Adults or older youth can play the parts of the Choir Director, Mohr, Gruber, and the Austrian Choir, while the "Singer" parts can be played by upper-elementary school children.

The play incorporates music into the story line, and all cast members will sing within the play. An offstage choir can supplement the singing, if desired. The play also requires a guitar player. Ideally, the actor playing the part of Gruber would also be a guitarist. But, if that's not possible, he can pretend to play while a real guitarist performs offstage.

One of several "play rehearsal" plays in this volume, "Love Finds A Way" requires no set, and no costumes except for choir robes and some wool scarves. Simple theatrical lighting would enhance the transition from the present to the past, but a simple "on" and "off" flick of a light switch can suffice.

(As the play opens, the littlest members of the Sunday school are performing a song. They begin to leave down the center aisle, as the actors playing members of the youth choir come in from stage right dressed in their robes. It's the morning of Christmas Eve and they are having their final rehearsal before singing a big anthem at tonight's service. They are standing stage left. All are excited.)

Singer 1: *(watching the little ones leave)* Good, they're done. Now we can practice.

Singer 2: I can't wait to do our song tonight. Everybody in my family is coming!

Singer 3: Even my daddy's coming, and he never goes to church.

Singer 4: This is my first time singing in front of everybody. I'm kinda' scared.

Singer 5: *(a little bit older and a bit of a brat)* Nothing to worry about. It's not hard at all.

Singer 3: Where's our director? Shouldn't we start practicing?

Singer 2: She was here before. I saw her doing something with the piano.

Singer 1: Yeah. Somebody else was here, too; some guy with a tool kit.

Singer 4: You don't think ...

Singer 5: *(with a lot of mock confidence)* God's not gonna let anything happen that can't be fixed. We're doing this for him, right?

All Singers: *(muttering with mock bravado)* Yeah, sure, that's right ...

Assistant Choir Director: *(enters from stage right)* I've got some really bad news. The piano is broken.

All Singers: Oh, no. It can't be ...

Singer 1: What are we gonna do?

Singer 2: *(angry and hurt)* What can we do? All that work, for nothing.

Singer 3: My daddy will be so disappointed.

Singer 4: I may never get to sing.

Singer 5: How could God do this?

Assistant Choir Director: Don't blame God. Blame the mice.

Singer 2: Mice?

Assistant Choir Director: Yeah. Mice got into the piano and chewed up the little felt pads inside. It will just take too much time to replace all those pads by tonight.

Singer 3: Can't we try?

All: Please?

Assistant Choir Director: We did try. There's nothing they can do today. Look, maybe we can sing the anthem next Sunday.

Singer 2: Christmas will be over by then. What a crummy service this is going to be with no music.

(Choir Director comes in holding several pieces of sheet music.)

Singer 3: What are we gonna do?

Choir Director: We're going to sing, of course.

Singer 5: But how? We can't sing without the piano.

Choir Director: Don't need the piano. We can use something else.

Singer 2: But we won't sound good without the piano.

Choir Director: A long time ago, another church had a problem like this and they found a way to have music. Just like we're going to do.

Singer 5: I suppose you're going to tell us the story.

Singer 1: *(tapping Singer 5 on the head with the sheet music)* Don't be nasty. *(to Choir Director)* Please, tell us.

Choir Director: Okay — the year was 1818, and the place was Obendorf, Austria. It was Christmas Eve and the assistant pastor, who was new to the church, had just told the organist that the organ was broken.

(Lights should dim a bit. All "present" choir people move off left. Mohr and Gruber enter from stage right. Mohr stands on the platform. Gruber sits on the edge of the stage nervously fingering a guitar.)

Mohr: Mice, can you believe it, Franz? Mice decided to make nests in the organ pipes. The repairmen said there's nothing they can do before tonight's service.

Gruber: But the choir. They prepared such a beautiful anthem. How disappointed they're going to be.

Mohr: Not just the choir. This isn't going to look too good for either of us.

Gruber: I know. Father will have a fit. We've never had a service without music.

Mohr: I thought of something ...

Gruber: What? I'm open to suggestions.

Mohr: *(shyly producing the poem from his pocket)* I wrote this little poem. I thought maybe you could write music for it.

Gruber: And what? Make the choir sing without accompaniment?

Mohr: *(points to guitar)* I thought maybe you could write the music for that.

Gruber: A guitar anthem? On Christmas Eve?

Mohr: I know it sounds crazy, and I know you don't have much time, but what choice do we have?

Gruber: *(looking at the words)* "Silent Night, Holy Night." Pretty words. All right, Joseph. I'll give it a shot.

(Gruber and Mohr exit. Lights fade down quickly. Offstage guitarist should be in position. Mohr and the Austrian Choir, wearing the same robes as contemporary choir, but with a wool scarf knotted around their throats, enters from stage right, grumbling much the same as their contemporary equivalents.)

Gruber: *(entering from right with guitar and sheet music)* Okay. By now you all know the organ is broken, so we have to do something a little different. Pastor Mohr and I wrote this song. *(hands music to first choir member, who passes it on to the others)*

Austrian Choir Member 1: You expect us to learn a new song for tonight?

Austrian Choir Member 2: That's crazy!

Austrian Choir Member 3: Besides, what are we going to sing with?

Gruber: *(touching guitar)* This. Yeah. I know its crazy, but it's all we've got ...

Mohr: Please, just try it.

Austrian Choir Member 4: I'll try it, but I don't like it.

Austrian Choir Member 1: Shut up and sing.

(Gruber plays the introduction and the choir, rather haltingly, sings the first verse of "Silent Night" in German. [Note: Don't worry if the children struggle with the German. Remember, within the context of the play, it's the first time the Austrian Choir is singing the song. It shouldn't sound perfect.] After finishing the German verse, the contemporary choir and the little ones that sang at the beginning of the play don scarves and join the Austrian Choir to sing the first verse in English. As the last notes fade, lights dim slightly.)

Mohr and Gruber: Amen.

Austrian Choir Member 1: That was beautiful!

(Lights dim further. The little ones and Gruber and Mohr exit stage right. All choir members remove scarves. Austrian Choir members now become late-arriving contemporary choir members.)

Austrian Choir Member 1: Sorry we're late.

Austrian Choir Member 2: Did we miss anything?

Singer 2: A wonderful story!

Singer 5: That and a broken piano. What happened when the choir sang the song?

Choir Director: You should all know what happened. "Silent Night" has become one of the world's favorite Christmas carols. We sing it every year. So, you see, God does find a way.

Singer 5: *(to Singer 4)* See, I told you!

Assistant Choir Director: Love found a way. The same love that made God send us Jesus as a little baby. The same love we celebrate each Christmas. I'm sorry I thought it was hopeless. *(grinning)* Let me guess. We're going to do the same thing, right?

Choir Director: Right. I've picked out this song, which is written for guitar and choir, and I found someone in the Senior Choir who plays.

(Gruber, minus the scarf, enters from right and sits on the edge of the platform with guitar.)

Singer 3: Can we learn it in time?

Assistant Choir Director: Why not?

Singer 5: If those Austrians could learn a new song in time, so can we.

(Choir Director passes out music to contemporary anthem and the children sing.)

Singer 5: I think God did it again.

All: Amen!

It Wasn't The Hilton, You Know

Characters (in order of appearance)

Child 1 (Lead Shepherd) — Ryan   Director — Iian
Child 2 (Mary) — Calee   Assistant Director — Carson
Child 3 (Narrator) — Juri   Kristy (Innkeeper's Wife) — Flower
Child 4 (Joseph) — Jordan   Shepherd 2 — Garrett
Child 5 (Lead Angel) — Taylor   Shepherd 3 — Makenzie
Child 6 (Angel 2) — Rion

Props

Dish towels
Bathrobes
White pillow cases
Cardboard box
Stuffed animals — a few
Piece of white fabric
"Scripts"
Broom
Clipboard
Tinsel halos
Cardboard star
Baby doll
Baby blanket

Notes

This play about doing a play drives home the central message of this volume — that the trappings of the Christmas holiday, including those of the church Christmas play or pageant, often are allowed to outweigh the message. Ideal for small Sunday schools, the play has only eleven speaking parts, as all the children are actors in the play-within-a-play. The Director and Assistant Director should be played by adults or older youth. The balance of the parts can be played by children of any age. And, since its setting is a play rehearsal in a church a week before Christmas, it requires no set, and the only costumes and props are the ones listed above in the Props section.

(As the play opens, a group of children are sitting and standing around the front of the sanctuary. Some are studying lines. The smaller ones are playing with the stuffed animal props. No one looks happy.)

Child 1: *(looking at watch)* Well, she's late ... again.

Child 2: What else is new? Anyway, what's one more rehearsal? It's not going to help this show.

Child 3: Why? I thought we sounded pretty good last week. Everyone knew their lines ... Well, almost everyone. *(looking at Child 4)*

Child 4: It's the stupid dish towel. I can't think with it on.

Child 2: That's it. It's the dishtowels and the bathrobes. And, the pillow cases on the little angels. Who cares about some dumb lines when the show looks so ... cheesy?

Child 4: Tell me about it. At least you get a real dress.

Child 2: Since when do you want a dress?

Child 4: You know what I mean. You wear real clothes.

Child 5: *(holding up a cardboard box with a doll inside)* And they call this a manger.

Child 6: At my friend's church, they have a real wooden stable, and every year they have a real baby to play Jesus. And, this year, they're using real animals. They're going to have a sheep and a cow.

Child 4: Bet that place will smell really good.

Child 3: Hey, remember, that church is a lot bigger than ours.

Child 1: And has more money.

Child 2: Yeah. That's the whole problem here. You can't do a decent show without the bucks.

(Director runs in from left, followed by the Assistant Director, who is practically invisible because of the mounds of costume pieces she's carrying. She drops the costumes onto the stage and sits on the edge. During the next scene, she separates the costume pieces into piles for Shepherds, Angels, and so on.)

Director: Sorry I'm late. I was out looking for something that might make a better manger *(shrugs shoulder)*, but no luck.

Child 2: *(grabbing a piece of white fabric from the pile)* Okay, I surrender. Let's just forget this play.

Director: *(picking up the box)* Look, it's not that bad. We'll cover it with some brown paper.

Assistant Director: Maybe we could get some hay to put inside.

Child 4: It will still be a box. And, if I have to wear that dish towel again, I quit.

Child 5: Me, too. Let's go.

Director: Hang on a second. Is that what you think this is all about? Who has the best costume? What church can smell the most like a stable? Have any of you actually read your scripts?

Child 3: I did. Do you want to hear my big monologue from page three?

Assistant Director: Not again, please.

Director: I'm not talking about your individual parts. I mean have you read the whole story?

All Children: *(at the same time, each with a different excuse)* Well ... not really ... I had a lot of homework ... My baby sister tore up my script....

Director: Okay. Let's walk through the play right now. And I want you to really listen ... and not just for your cues, though you could all use some work on that. Listen to what everybody else is saying and see if you can't find the real meaning of this story.

(Assistant Director sweeps costumes off the stage and begins handing pieces to each of the actors. Child 3, who is the Narrator in the play, takes her place at the podium. Assistant Director picks up a clipboard and moves to stage left to cue the actors. Director takes a seat in the front row of the auditorium.)

Child 3 (Narrator): Start now?

Director: Whenever you're ready.

Child 3 (Narrator): I'm always ready. Where should I start?

Director: With Mary and Joseph's entrance. *(points to Child 2 and Child 4)* From back there. Let's do it like it's for real ... and I do mean real.

(Child 2 and Child 4 walk to the back of the church and then slowly begin walking down the center aisle.)

Child 2 (Mary): *(emoting heavily)* Joseph. I can't go any further. I'm so tired, and I'm thirsty, and I've got a pebble in my sandal.

Director: Please. No improvisation. The play is running long as is.

Child 2 (Mary): You said you wanted it real. I'm sure Mary said more than "I'm tired."

Director: But she didn't have ten baby angels running up and down the aisles.

Child 2 (Mary): Sorry. *(back in character)* We have to find a place to sleep.

Child 4 (Joseph): *(wearing a dish towel)* I've been trying, Mary. But, all the inns are full. Nobody has any room.

Child 2 (Mary): Surely there is a warm and dry place somewhere.

Child 3 (Narrator): Finally, they came to a small inn on a side road. Even this simple place was completely filled. But the Innkeeper, seeing how tired Mary was, took pity on them and offered the use of his stable.

Assistant Director: We still haven't cast the part of the Innkeeper. Greg was going to do it, but his folks decided to go skiing for the Christmas holidays.

Director: Well, who in the chorus hasn't gotten a part yet?

Assistant Director: *(looking at the cast off left)* Kristy.

Kristy: I'm not putting on a robe and a ratty beard to play an Innkeeper. No way.

Director: Don't worry about that. We can't afford another ratty beard. So, put on a robe and be the Innkeeper's Wife.

Kristy: Okay. What do I have to say?

Assistant Director: *(handing her a script and pointing to the lines)* Start with "We have no room...."

Kristy: *(to Joseph)* We have no rooms to offer.

Child 4 (Joseph): Please, my wife can't go on. We've walked all day and she is very close to having our first child.

Kristy: Well, there's the stable. It's warm, and it's a lot cleaner than some of the other inns in this town.

Child 2 (Mary): That will do fine.

Director: How many of you have ever seen a stable? Or smelled one? It wasn't the Hilton, you know. Okay. Let's take a look at the shepherd scene.

(Mary and Joseph take their places downstage center. Shepherds enter from left and group themselves on the floor in front of the stage. Assistant Director gathers the Angels offstage left, preparing them for their entrance.)

Child 3 (Narrator): In the fields outside of Bethlehem, a group of shepherds were watching their sheep. Suddenly, the sky grew very bright.

Child 5 (Lead Angel): *(entering from left, tinsel halo somewhat askew)* Fear not. We bring you good news. Unto us a child is born. His name is Jesus and he has come to save us all from our sins.

Child 3 (Narrator): Then, a whole group of angels appeared, praising God and saying:

(All angels, including the little ones, enter from left and stand with Child 5.)

All Angels: Glory to God in the highest. Peace on Earth. Good will toward men.

Child 6 (Angel 2): Why do we have to say those lines every year?

Assistant Director: *(nodding toward the Director)* I think she just likes them.

Director: It's in the original script. You know, the Bible? Besides, it's something simple enough for the little ones to say each year. And yes, I do like those words. It's the whole reason for celebrating Christmas. It is important we all understand the words.

Child 6 (Angel 2): *(shrugging shoulders)* Just asking.

(Assistant Director herds the Angels back off left. Shepherds stand up.)

Child 3 (Narrator): As the angels left, the shepherds were filled with wonder. They decided to look for this special child.

Child 1 (Lead Shepherd): What are we waiting for? Let's find the child.

Shepherd 2: I bet he's in Bethlehem. It's the closest town to here.

Shepherd 3: I wonder where in the city he'll be?

Child 1 (Lead Shepherd): Someplace fancy, I bet. Look, that funny star we saw before is moving. Maybe it will take us to the baby.

(Assistant Director hands cardboard star to one of the Angels, who marches down the center aisle of the church. The Shepherds follow. They loop around the back of the church and then return up the left aisle to center stage where Mary and Joseph are sitting. Assistant Director plops baby doll back into a hastily covered manger. Mary and Joseph back up a bit to make room for the Shepherds to stand on either side of them.)

Child 3 (Narrator): The shepherds followed the star, and there they found the Baby Jesus in the most unusual place.

Child 1 (Lead Shepherd): Please, is the baby here?

Shepherd 2: The baby the angels talked about?

Child 2 (Mary): Yes, he is here. His name is Jesus. Please come closer.

Shepherd 2: But the angels said he had come to save our sins. This little guy, he can't even keep himself warm.

Shepherd 3: Why is he here? He should be in a palace.

Child 4 (Joseph): God didn't want him to come as a king. *(looks over at the Director)* I think I just got the message.

Director: That's why I asked if you'd read the play. The message is right there. If Jesus had come as a king, if he'd been born in a palace and swaddled in furs, his message would have only gone to the rich and powerful.

Child 2 (Mary): *(removing her Mary dish towel headdress)* But, he wanted it to go to all of us. So, he came to this world as one of us.

Director: Exactly. I know you'd like the costumes and sets for this play to be a lot prettier. I would, too. But, let's not get wrapped up in all the trappings. Because, we don't need them. All we need is the message.

Child 5: So, I guess the type of manger really doesn't matter.

Child 3: This box is probably just as a good as a crummy wooden manger ... maybe even a little nicer.

Child 1: And I bet our bathrobes are a lot warmer and a lot cleaner than the stuff those poor shepherds wore.

Child 6: I still wish we could use real animals.

Assistant Director: *(picking up a stuffed sheep)* Trust me. These smell a lot better.

Director: So, you'll still do the play?

Child 4: Sure. If Jesus could be born next to sheep, I guess I can stand a dish towel.

Director: Next year, I'll upgrade you all to scarves. I promise. For now, let's rehearse your curtain call.

(All the children return to the stage, Child 2 and 4 at the center. They join hands and bow as Director applauds.)

If We Do It, It Will Work

Characters (in order of appearance)

God (offstage voice)	Shepherd 1
Gabriel	Shepherd 2
Michael	Shepherd 3
Mary	Shepherd 4
Messenger	Angel 1
Joseph	Angel 2
Innkeeper	Angel 3
Innkeeper's Wife	Angel 4
Lead Shepherd	Angel 5

Props

Paper (decree)
Arrow sign saying "To Bethlehem"

Notes

No one really knows much about the personality of the angels Gabriel and Michael. "If We Do It, It Will Work" takes some dramatic license in assigning personalities for these characters, portraying them as something of an "odd couple." It views Gabriel as a "by-the-book" worrier, and Michael as more of a laid-back type. If possible, Gabriel's robe should fit perfectly and be spotless. Michael's should be open and he should wear his halo backward or tilted to one side.

Other than the two leads, roles in this play have few lines with no big words, making this an excellent play for younger children. Gabriel and Michael should be played by youth or adults. "God," who is heard, but never seen in the play, ideally should be voiced by an adult.

The play calls for one "lighting effect," a pinpoint spot to symbolize the star. If theatrical lighting is not available, a similar effect can be achieved by dimming the sanctuary lights, and placing someone in the front row with a small flashlight.

(Stage is empty as the play begins. The person reading the part of God will be stationed in the choir loft, or off to one side of the stage, with a microphone.)

God: Gabriel, Gabriel. Where are you? Come on, there's work to be done.

Gabriel: *(rushes in from right, adjusting robe)* All right, all right, I'm coming. What's the rush? Oh. I'm sorry, sir. I didn't know it was you.

Michael: *(enters left)* What's up?

God: Glad you could join us, Michael. Well, it's time.

Michael: For what?

Gabriel: You don't mean ... IT?

God: Yes, IT.

Gabriel: But, we're not ready yet. There's still so much to be done.

God: Relax. Take a deep breath ... *(Gabriel and Michael both inhale and exhale noisily. Each then sits, one on each side of the stage)* good. Now, believe me. The time is right. Everything is going according to the plan. *(to Gabriel)* You spoke to Mary, right?

(Mary enters from left, and stands on platform stage left, facing out.)

Gabriel: Of course. I told her just what you said. "Fear not, Mary, for thou hast found favor with God. And, behold, you shall bring forth a son, and shall call his name Jesus." She was a little confused at first, but then she was very happy.

Mary: *(to audience)* My soul doth magnify the Lord. And, my spirit hath rejoiced in God, my Savior. For he hath regarded the low estate of his handmaiden. For, behold, from henceforth, all generations will call me blessed. *(Mary exits left.)*

God: So, she's ready. And, Joseph?

Michael: He was kind of upset. He even thought about not marrying Mary, but I popped in to see him — woke him up in the middle of the night. He got the message.

God: You're both doing a fine job. Now, relax and I'll talk you through the rest of it. This is exactly what you do. First, we get them to Bethlehem.

Michael: But they live in Nazareth. How do we get them to Bethlehem?

(Messenger walks across the front of the stage with a large decree [paper]. Stops center stage.)

Messenger: The great Caesar Augustus declares that all people must return to their hometown to be counted and taxed. This must be done NOW.

(Messenger exits right. Reenters with an arrow sign that says "To Bethlehem," pointing to center stage. Messenger stands at front while Mary and Joseph enter from the back of the church and begin walking up center aisle. Once they reach the front, Messenger exits right.)

Gabriel: *(to Michael)* How did he do that?

God: I'm God! It's all part of the plan.

Mary: We've been walking so long, Joseph. Can't we find any place to stay?

Joseph: We've tried just about every inn in town. Everyone's here to pay the taxes.

Mary: The baby will be coming soon.

Joseph: It looks like there's a place just up the road. I'll try to talk the innkeeper into giving us something.

(Innkeeper enters from left and stands on platform, center stage.)

Michael: This is great. Bring everyone to town at once so there are no rooms. Now, where are we going to put them?

God: Just watch.

Joseph: *(talking to Innkeeper)* Please, sir. We've walked a long while. My wife is so tired.

Innkeeper: I'm sorry. But we have no rooms.

(Innkeeper's Wife enters from left and crosses to Innkeeper.)

Innkeeper's Wife: What about the barn out back? It's warm and clean.

Innkeeper: Sure, you can use the barn if you'd like.

Joseph: Thank you. We'll take it.

Innkeeper's Wife: *(to Innkeeper)* You take them back there. I'll get them some blankets and bring out something for them to eat.

Michael: I don't believe it. He did it again.

God: Believe it. Now we have to let people know.

Gabriel: Right, I'll go let Herod know, and Michael can alert the leaders of the temple. What kind of sign are you going to give them this time? Are you going to part a sea? Turn water into blood? I hope its not locusts again.

God: Slow down. Nothing that flashy. I just want you to bring in the star.

Gabriel: A star?

God: Yes, a bright and shining star no one's ever seen before. Bring it on.

(A pinpoint spot beams a light on the wall. Gabriel "directs" its placement.)

Gabriel: No, move it a bit to the left. Now back to the right. Now up a little. Perfect.

Michael: Now, we go tell Herod, right?

God: Not Herod. Not yet, anyway. There are some shepherds over in the next field. I want you to get the other angels and tell them.

Gabriel: But if we don't bring your message to Herod or someone like that, how are we going to prove that the Son of God has come?

Michael: How will we get them to follow you and to stop the bad stuff they're doing?

God: I have my reasons. Let's just say, this message has to come from the ground up.

(Shepherds enter from left and sit on the floor in the center.)

Lead Shepherd: Look at the sky. It's so clear and bright tonight.

Shepherd 1: Wait, what's that?

Lead Shepherd: I don't know. *(nudges other Shepherds)* Wake up and look at this.

Shepherd 2: I've never seen that star before.

Shepherd 3: It's so big and shiny!

(Off left, Gabriel and Michael round up the Angels, most of whom are NOT ready to go on.)

Angel 1: Why didn't you tell us sooner?

Gabriel: We just found out.

Angel 2: But what's the rush?

Michael: We've got to talk to these shepherds before they get scared and run away.

Angel 3: Shepherds? You said we'd be appearing to the King.

Gabriel: Do you want to argue with him? *(Points up toward God. Angel 3 shakes her head)*

Angel 4: Wait for me.

(Gabriel and Michael get Angels organized back of center stage.)

Gabriel: Okay. Now, just like we rehearsed it.

(First Angel steps forward. Shepherds pull away.)

Lead Shepherd: Uh, oh. This is getting really weird.

Shepherd 1: Look at that.

Shepherd 3: I don't want to.

Shepherd 4: Quick, hide the sheep.

Michael: Relax, we don't want your sheep. *(to Angel 1)* Go ahead, tell them.

Angel 1: Fear not, for behold I bring you glad tidings of great joy.

Angel 2: For unto you is born this day in the city of David, a Savior which is Christ the Lord.

Angel 3: And this shall be a sign unto you: You shall find the baby wrapped in swaddling clothes and lying in a manger.

All Angels: Glory to God in the highest, and Peace on Earth, good will to men.

God: Not bad. That was a nice touch.

Gabriel: Thanks. I have my moments.

Michael: Well, it was my idea to have the little angels.

God: Now, now. We don't have time for this. Michael, the little angels were good, too.

Michael: Thanks.

Angel 3: Can we go now?

Gabriel: Oh, yeah. Good job. Take a break.

(Angels exit, except for Angels 4 and 5.)

Shepherd 4: Let's go see the baby now.

Lead Shepherd: But we can't just leave the sheep. *(looking at Gabriel)* Or can we?

Gabriel: They'll be fine.

Angel 4: I'll watch them.

Angel 5: Me, too.

(Angels 4 and 5 pick up sheep and carry them off left.)

Lead Shepherd: Well then, let's go.

(Shepherds exit left.)

Gabriel: Okay, so the shepherds know, and they've gone to see the baby. But how far can they take your message?

God: Farther than you might think. Oh, by the way, some powerful people already know about the birth. See the way the star is moving? Some very wise kings from a far-off land have already seen that star and are following it. It will be some time before they get here, but when they do, they will tell Herod.

Michael: It's about time. So, then Herod will change his ways and treat the people better?

Gabriel: Or, maybe he'll just move out of the palace and let Jesus move in, like he should?

God: No, I'm afraid he won't do either. Herod will be so jealous of Jesus, he'll do everything he can to hurt him. But before he can get near Jesus, Michael will warn Joseph, who'll take Mary and the baby away to Egypt.

Michael: No problem. After this, that'll be easy.

Gabriel: *(very proud)* Well, we really pulled that off, didn't we?

God: Just remember, this is only the beginning.

Gabriel: But he's here. We'll keep him safe.

Michael: Then, when he grows up, he'll tell everyone about you.

Gabriel: What else is there?

God: Bringing him here wasn't really the point. It's what he still has to do that matters. They won't know what he's done until he's gone. And that is the point.

Michael: I'm confused.

Gabriel: There's still a lot I don't understand.

God: That's why I gave you faith. So you can believe in what you don't understand. Oh, by the way, Merry Christmas.

Michael: Christmas?

Gabriel: What's that?

God: The way in which people will remember this day thousands of years from now.

Gabriel: Oh *(to Michael)*, Merry Christmas.

Michael: *(to audience)* Merry Christmas.

(If stage lighting is available, there should be a quick blackout. When the lights come back up, the cast comes out and takes a bow.)

Christmas Eve At Angel School

Characters (in order of appearance)

Teacher Angel	Lead Shepherd
1st Angel	Shepherd 1
2nd Angel	Shepherd 2
3rd Angel	Shepherd 3
4th Angel	1st Child
5th Angel	2nd Child
Joseph	3rd Child
Mary	4th Child
Angel Choir	5th Child

Props

Chairs
Blackboard with "Junior Angel Training" written on it
Lectern or music stand
Christmas tree
Christmas tree decorations
4 Bibles
Manger, with a baby

"Christmas Eve At Angel School" offers a variety of speaking roles for children of all ages, making it a good choice for medium-sized Sunday schools or churches. There are two different "set" areas. Stage left is the "classroom." Several small chairs are arranged in a half-circle. A blackboard, on which is written "Junior Angel Training," is placed at the back of the stage behind the chairs. A lectern or music stand is placed downstage left, facing the chairs.

At the end of the play, there is a short scene in which children are decorating a Christmas tree. If there is no tree in the performance space, a small one can be set on the end of the platform stage right.

(As the play begins, several small Angels and one or two slightly older Angels enter from left and take a seat in the classroom. The Teacher Angel enters carrying a Bible and takes place in front of lectern.)

Teacher Angel: Okay. Settle down. We've got a lot to do today.

1st Angel: I'm still not sure why we have to go to school.

Teacher Angel: To understand God's plan and how we fit into it.

2nd Angel: *(a bit of a wise guy)* But I didn't think we had to do anything, except fly around and be happy.

Teacher Angel: God has given us a special job. We were created to sing praises to him and to bring his message of love to the world.

2nd Angel: That doesn't sound so special to me.

Teacher Angel: Oh, but it is! You're too young to remember, but there have been many times in the past when God has chosen us to spread his good news to mankind.

All Angels: *(ad libs)* When? What did we do? Really?

Teacher Angel: We protected Daniel in the lions' den. And we were present in the burning bush when God told Moses to go to Egypt.

3rd Angel: And, don't forget the first Christmas.

Teacher Angel: Right. People might never have known that our Savior had been born if it hadn't been for us.

4th Angel: Well, that star helped a little. But, I'll never forget that night.

All Angels: *(ad libs)* Well, what happened? What star? Tell us the story!

Teacher Angel: Okay, okay. But I'm going to need some help. *(points to 3rd, 4th, and 5th Angels)* Now, really pay attention to what we tell you, and we just might be able to show you what happened on that special night.

(The three Angels move to the other side of the platform. Each holds a Bible.)

Teacher Angel: *(reading from Bible)* And it came to pass in those days that there went out a decree from Caesar Augustus that all the world should be taxed. And all went out, everyone unto his own city ...

2nd Angel: What does "taxed" mean?

Teacher Angel: It means everyone had to pay money to the leader.

3rd Angel: And Joseph went up from Galilee, out of the city of Nazareth into Judea, unto the city of David, which is called Bethlehem, because he was of the house and lineage of David.

2nd Angel: What does "lineage" mean?

Teacher Angel: You know, you ask an awful lot of questions.

1st Angel: Let her tell the story, please.

(Mary and Joseph enter from center aisle.)

Joseph: Come on, Mary. Just a little bit further.

Mary: I'm so tired. I just want to rest.

Joseph: Surely some inn has room for us.

4th Angel: *(to the children)* But, they never did find an inn. They ended up sleeping in a stable that night.

All Angels: Yuck!

4th Angel: *(reading again)* And while they were there, she brought forth her firstborn son and wrapped him in swaddling clothes and laid him in a manger.

(Mary and Joseph reach the front and perch on the end of the platform, between the "school" and the Angels telling the story. 5th Angel crosses to Mary and hands her a "manger" holding the Baby, which Mary settles next to her. Standing over Mary and Joseph, the 5th Angel takes up the narration. As soon as 5th Angel begins to speak, Shepherds should enter from stage left and curl up in a circle on the floor in front of the platform.)

5th Angel: And there were in the same country, shepherds abiding in the field, keeping watch over their flocks by night. And, lo, the Angel of the Lord came upon them. *(looks out toward audience)* That was me. They were very afraid and I said, "Fear not. For behold I bring you good tidings of great joy, which shall be to all people. For unto you is born this day, in the city of David, a Savior, which is Christ the Lord. And this shall be a sign unto you, ye shall find the baby wrapped in swaddling clothes and lying in a manger."

(5th Angel moves right back to the other Angel narrators, very pleased with herself. 3rd Angel crosses left back to the "school" and gets all the Angel children to stand. Then she steps off the platform and stands stage left to "conduct" the children.)

3rd Angel: And suddenly it was with the angels, a multitude of the heavenly hosts, praising God and saying: *(to children)* Okay, just like we rehearsed it.

All Angels: Glory to God in the highest. Peace on Earth, good will toward men.

(Narrator Angels applaud. Then 3rd Angel directs the children to sit and later they return to the classroom.)

Lead Shepherd: Hey, let's go to Bethlehem and see this wonder that God has made known to us.

Shepherd 1: But, what about the sheep?

Shepherd 2: Oh, just leave them. I think God will watch them.

Lead Shepherd: Right. On this holy and special night, I'm sure they will be perfectly safe right here.

4th Angel: *(coming down off the platform)* I'll take care of them.

Shepherd 3: Have you ever watched sheep before?

4th Angel: No, but it can't be any tougher than watching them. *(points to little Angels)*

Shepherd 2: You see. I told you God would take care of them tonight.

Lead Shepherd: So, what are we waiting for?

(Shepherds, Mary, and Joseph exit stage left. 3rd, 4th, and 5th Angels, along with Teacher Angel, go back to "classroom," the 4th Angel stopping first to pick up the sheep.)

1st Angel: Wow! That was something. Do you suppose I'll ever get a chance to tell God's story like that?

Teacher Angel: If you listen very carefully to what God has to say, and follow him, then God will find a way to use you.

2nd Angel: But God doesn't let us appear in the sky singing his praises like that anymore.

Teacher Angel: No. But you don't need to be loud and flashy. Sometimes the best way to tell God's message is in a whisper so soft and gentle you can only hear it in your heart. *(checks watch)* Oh dear, if you don't hurry, you'll all be late for your flying lessons. Hurry now.

(All Angels exit stage left except for 1st Angel, who sits on the end of the platform stage left. She stays there throughout the next scene.)

1st Angel: So soft and gentle you can only hear it in your heart. I don't understand. People don't hear with their hearts.

(Angels and Shepherds reenter from left without their costumes and move stage right to the Christmas tree. They pretend to be decorating the tree as they talk.)

1st Child: Boy, I love Christmas Eve.

2nd Child: And tomorrow's even better. I know I'm getting lots of toys this year.

3rd Child: Why?

2nd Child: Because I've been very good.

4th Child: Yeah, right.

2nd Child: No, really, I have.

4th Child: Then why was Mom yelling at you yesterday?

2nd Child: She wasn't yelling. She just had to talk loud to be heard over the vacuum cleaner ... 'cause I broke the "off" button. It was an accident, I swear!

5th Child: I hope I get a lot of stuff. But, you know, the best part really is having the whole family together.

1st Child: I guess we're finished with the tree.

4th Child: It looks really good. Hey, let's go to my house for hot chocolate.

5th Child: *(to 3rd Child)* Are you coming?

3rd Child: No, I don't think so.

1st Child: Why not? You'll miss, all the fun.

5th Child: What's the matter?

3rd Child: I picked a fight with my sister over something stupid ... who would ride in the front seat when we went to pick up Grandma at the station. I said some awful things, like I wish she wasn't my sister. I made her cry. I don't think she wants to spend Christmas with me.

2nd Child: Oh, she's just being a grouch. Let's go.

(All children exit up center aisle except for 3rd Child, who sits on platform stage right. 1st Angel stands up on platform, picks up one of the Bibles left by the older Angels, and begins to read.)

1st Angel: "For unto you is born a Savior...."

(Teacher Angel enters from left and walks to 1st Angel.)

Teacher Angel: "... who is Christ the Lord. And they called his name Jesus for he came to save his people from their sins ..."

(1st Angel is now right behind the 3rd Child. She bends over and pretends to whisper in her ear.)

1st Angel: ... including making your sister cry. Tell her you're sorry.

3rd Child: *(as if an idea has just come to her)* If I tell her I'm sorry, she'll forgive me. Then we can have Christmas together! *(yelling off left to her friends)* Hey, wait up! I want hot chocolate, too.

(3rd Child exits off left. Teacher Angel goes up to 1st Angel and throws an arm around her shoulder.)

Teacher Angel: You just gave her the best present of all. A reminder that Jesus came as a baby to provide forgiveness for all the bad things we do.

1st Angel: It's Jesus' present. I just delivered it.

Teacher Angel: I told you. God has a plan for all of us. We just have to listen for his voice, no matter how softly it comes.

1st Angel: *(to Teacher Angel)* Merry Christmas.

Teacher Angel: Peace on Earth. Good will toward men.

(The two exit left.)

Room At The Inn

Characters (in order of appearance)

Narrator	Shepherd 2
Innkeeper	Other Shepherds (nonspeaking)
Innkeeper's Wife	Angel 1
Mary	Angel 2
Joseph	Angel 3
Shepherd 1	Innkeeper's Daughter

Props
- Chair
- Brush
- Lantern
- Manger
- Baby doll

Notes

With only eleven speaking parts, many of the roles are only a line or two in length, and a very basic set, "Room At The Inn" is a fairly simple play to stage. The set consists of one chair, placed stage left, facing out. A lantern is placed at the end of stage left.

(Narrator stands at a lectern placed upstage right.)

Narrator: On an unusually quiet street in the town of Bethlehem sat a small inn that had seen better days. It had only six rooms for rent. A small barn stood behind it, housing three cows, an old horse, and a dozen or so sheep. Doves nested in the rafters above. Fresh hay had been laid in the manger for the animals to graze.

Normally, very few people stayed at this inn. But the government had ordered a census, and people had flocked to town. All the better inns filled up quickly. So, little by little, the people came, and it was well after midnight by the time the Innkeeper had seen the last tired couple to their room.

(Innkeeper's Wife enters stage left. She sits in the chair and begins to brush her hair. The Innkeeper enters, stretching his neck and shoulders. Both are very tired.)

Innkeeper: Well, I got the last of them put away for the night. It's been ages since we've been this full.

Innkeeper's Wife: At least it means we'll be able to pay the bills this month.

Innkeeper: Yes, the census has been good for business. I can't believe how many people are in town.

(Mary and Joseph enter up center aisle. At the front, they stop just short of where the Innkeeper and his wife stand. Joseph pantomimes a knock at the door.)

Innkeeper: Who could that be now? *(pantomimes opening the door)*

Joseph: Brother Innkeeper, do you have a room for the night?

Innkeeper: No, we're full up. Go away. *(pantomimes starting to shut the door)*

Joseph: *(with some desperation)* No, please. My wife is about to have our first child. We've traveled so far and there's just no room at any other inn. Please, don't send us back out into the night.

(Innkeeper's Wife comes to the door and looks with pity on Mary.)

Innkeeper's Wife: Ezra. Have you forgotten the basic rules of hospitality? She's about to have a baby. Surely we can find some place for them.

Innkeeper: Well, the stable is clean. I checked it myself this morning. There's plenty of fresh hay to rest on and I think there's one extra blanket in the closet. It's not much, but you're welcome to it.

Joseph: We'll take it, gladly. At least Mary will be able to get some sleep.

Innkeeper: Let me get a lantern and lead you out there.

(Innkeeper leads them off right. Shepherds enter from stage left and sit in a semicircle, center stage.)

Narrator: That same night shepherds were out in the fields nearby, watching over their flocks. Many were nodding off to sleep. All were huddled for warmth by a fire. One shepherd was staring up at the skies. He nudged his friend sleeping next to him.

Shepherd 1: Hey, look at that star.

Shepherd 2: You woke me up to see a star? Believe me. I've seen them all already.

Shepherd 1: But, you have to see this one. *(points up)* I've looked at the stars for years, too, but I've never seen anything like this.

Shepherd 2: *(staring up)* You're right. What do you think it is?

Shepherd 1: A shooting star, maybe?

Shepherd 2: But it's not falling. It's more like someone is guiding it. Pulling it by its tail to somewhere important.

Narrator: As the shepherds looked up, a band of angels appeared in the sky.

(Angels enter from left and stand on front part of platform.)

Shepherd 1: It just gets weirder.

Shepherd 2: And you were worried about a star?

(All Shepherds are now awake. They huddle together in fear.)

Angel 1: Fear not. For behold I bring you good tidings of great joy, which shall be to all people.

Angel 2: For unto you is born today, in the city of David, a Savior which is Christ the Lord.

Angel 3: And this shall be a sign unto you. You shall find the babe wrapped in swaddling clothes and lying in a manger.

Angel Choir: Glory to God in the highest. Peace on Earth, good will to men.

(Angels step down off platform, walk up the center aisle and exit out the back.)

Shepherd 1: A baby in a manger?

Shepherd 2: A Savior, which is Christ the Lord?

Shepherd 1: Hey, let's try to find this miraculous child.

Shepherd 2: But, they said he's in the city of David. I've never been to a city. Do you think it would be okay? I mean, look how we're dressed.

Shepherd 1: If this thing is as important as I think it is, we don't have time to worry about stuff like that. Let's go.

(Mary and Joseph reenter from stage right as Shepherds exit, following the Angels up the center aisle. Angels exit out through the back. Shepherds walk to the back, turn, and come back up to the front via the left aisle. Joseph carries the manger and sets it down on the platform center stage. Mary gently lays the baby in the manger. Innkeeper and wife peer through the imaginary door at left, and watch with some horror as the Shepherds approach.)

Innkeeper: What are those common shepherds doing here? Do those rules of hospitality mean I have to give them a room, too?

(Shepherds knock on imaginary door. Innkeeper pantomimes opening it just a crack.)

Innkeeper: I'm sorry. There are no rooms. Please take your flocks and go back to the valley.

Shepherd 1: We didn't come here for a room, sir. We've come to worship the miracle child.

Shepherd 2: Yes, we were told by the angels that this baby had been born in the city of David. I believe that's here — Bethlehem.

Shepherd 1: We've asked at every inn in town. Please, has the baby been born yet?

Innkeeper's Wife: The strangers in the stable? Perhaps she has had her child.

Innkeeper: You expect me to believe that tired, penniless young couple could have given birth to a miracle child?

Shepherd 1: Where is the stable? We must find out if the child is there.

Innkeeper: It's very late. And, I must say, I think it's very rude of you to be disturbing us at this hour. Tell me, how will you know if this is your miracle child?

Shepherd 2: The child the angels spoke of is the Son of God. I think we'll know if it is the right child by the love we'll see on his face.

Innkeeper's Wife: Honestly, Ezra, a miracle could be happening in your barn and all you care about is sleeping. I'll take you to the stable.

Innkeeper: *(reluctantly)* No. It's too late and I won't have you all scaring the cows. You shouldn't go back alone. Let me get the lantern.

(Innkeeper, Innkeeper's Wife, and Shepherds exit left and walk across the floor to the other side of the platform. The Innkeeper holds a lantern. The Shepherds look at child and immediately fall to their knees. Wife, hesitatingly, follows.)

Innkeeper: What are you kneeling for?

Innkeeper's Wife: I truly believe there is something special about this child. *(turning to Mary)* What is his name?

Mary: The angel told me to name him Jesus. I know it's kind of a strange name. But, he's been set apart for a special purpose.

Joseph: He's the promised Child of Light that will lead mankind out of the darkness, and reconcile humanity with its Creator.

Innkeeper: He's just been born and he's going to do all that? How can a little child save anyone? Nothing is as vulnerable or helpless as a baby.

Mary: But this child is the Son of God.

Innkeeper: How can he be the Son of God and your son, too? Are you a God?

Mary: No. Just someone who heard the Word, and listened, and believed. Just like these shepherds did. It's all part of his plan.

Joseph: As were you and your good wife when you took pity on weary strangers.

(Innkeeper's Daughter enters from stage left, rubbing her eyes.)

58

Daughter: Daddy, Mommy, did you hear the angels?

Innkeeper's Wife: *(going to the child and putting her arms around her)* Honey, what are you doing awake? Were we making too much noise?

Daughter: No, it was the angels. It was the sweetest music I've ever heard, and the happiest. Didn't you hear them?

Innkeeper's Wife: No, sweetie. We didn't. Tell me about it.

Daughter: I was sleeping when I heard this sound. Like the way you used to sing to me, only it was lots of voices singing all at once. And I looked out the window and the sky was so bright. After a while I could hear what they were singing about: a baby being born. And, then I heard the baby crying.

Mary: That was Jesus. Come see him. He's awake, too.

Daughter: I knew it. They sang of a baby, a marvelous baby, and here he is. Daddy, aren't we lucky? God chose to let him be born here.

Innkeeper's Wife: Yes, honey. God has truly blessed us.

Innkeeper: Now, wait a second. We welcome strangers. You hear some shepherds, who probably had gotten into the master's wine, singing, and all of a sudden we're part of a miracle? I think you've let all the excitement of this census get to you.

Daughter: Daddy, just look at the baby. Really look at him.

Innkeeper: What am I looking for? I see a child. A beautiful child. But, you were beautiful like that, too. Why is he so special?

Innkeeper's Wife: Think about the prophecies. All the years we've waited for something like this. Then, look at him again.

(Innkeeper looks down at the baby. This time he is really touched.)

Innkeeper: I'm not sure ... but, I think I see it now. Where's the blanket? I thought we had brought out a blanket for the baby?

Daughter: I'll get it, Daddy.

Innkeeper's Wife: And I'll reheat what was left of tonight's stew. Ezra, draw some fresh water for them.

Innkeeper: Yes. We'll do all of that and more for our special guests. But, first, I think we need to give thanks for the miracle of this night.

(Innkeeper kneels to pray. Lights fade down.)

Intermediate Plays

*A bit longer, a bit more challenging plays
for medium-sized casts of mixed age ranges*

Because God Said So, That's Why!

Characters (in order of appearance)

Narrator	Angel 2
David (or Rachel)	Angel 3
Esther	Angel 4
Shepherd 1	Angel Choir
Shepherd 2	King Caspar
Shepherd 3	King Balthazar
Shepherd 4	King Melchior
Shepherd 5	Mary
Lead Angel	Joseph

Props

Lectern or podium
Chair
Bundle with jar inside
Bundle with blanket inside
Gifts for the Wise Men to give to Jesus

Notes

This production can be restructured to suit a cast that is predominantly male or female. The lead part of David can easily be transformed to Rachel. In the original production, a girl did play this role.

The play offers roles for a wide range of ages. Adults or older youth could play the Kings, while upper elementary or "'tween" children can play the roles of David and Esther. The other roles are simple enough to be performed by younger elementary students.

The play is set right before the first Christmas. The place is somewhere out in the fields on the way to Bethlehem.

―――――――――――

(As the play begins, the stage is bare except for a lectern or podium off to the far stage right, with a chair for the Narrator to sit when he/she is not speaking.)

Narrator: This is a story about faith, a word you hear a lot in church. But how many of us know what faith really is? Or have ever done something on faith alone? Stepping out with only God's Word for proof can be scary. It can also take us to some amazing places.

That's the lesson David had to learn. He worked for King Melchior, one of the Wise Men who brought their gifts to Baby Jesus. David had been called in the middle of the night and told to pack for a long journey. His friend, Esther, had packed quickly without question. David lagged behind, complaining, and was barely ready on time. Now they had been walking for a long time and David had had enough.

(During the last part of the Narrator's speech, David and Esther enter stage right carrying bundles. They begin to walk across the stage. David stops halfway across, sets down his bundle, and sits on the edge of the platform. He takes off his shoes and begins rubbing his feet. Esther gets all the way across the stage, realizes that David isn't with her, and turns around.)

Esther: Why did you stop?

David: Because I'm tired. I can't walk another step.

Esther: This is the fifth time you've stopped today. We're so far back behind the others I can't even see the camels anymore.

David: I don't care. This whole thing is stupid.

Esther: It's not stupid. King Melchior says we're going to find a special child.

David: What special child? He can't tell us where the child is or what his name is. I don't think anyone knows where they are going. So, count me out. I've taken my last step.

Esther: King Melchior said God is leading us. And when we find the child, we'll know why it's important. You have to come. *(drops bundle and tries to pull David up)* Come on, you'll get us in trouble.

David: You don't have to stay with me. Go on if you're worried. I'm going to take a nap and then I'm headed back to the palace.

Esther: Go back? But you're carrying the myrrh, the most important thing.

(David pulls a jar out of bundle and hands it to Esther.)

David: Here. You take the stinky stuff. What can a baby do with it anyway? It's a dumb gift and this is a dumb trip. I'm staying here.

(Esther hesitates and when she sees David will not change his mind, she takes the myrrh. She pulls a blanket out of her bundle and hands it to David, then gently places the myrrh inside bundle.)

Esther: Here. It gets cold out here at night. Try to stay warm. I'll see you when we get back.

(David takes the blanket. Esther exits left. David watches her go, shaking his head and thinking how stupid she is to go. He then takes blanket and walks to the far left of the stage, curling up on the floor and pretending to go to sleep.)

Narrator: Not too far from where David slept, a group of shepherds, out watching their sheep, had just settled down for the night. They had built a fire and many of them were nodding off in sleep.

(Shepherds enter from back and come up center aisle during the Narrator's talk. They settle themselves center stage.)

Shepherd 1: *(nudging another shepherd who is falling asleep)* Will you wake up? You and I are supposed to be watching the sheep. I don't want to do it alone.

Shepherd 2: I can't help it. The fire is so warm and it's so quiet.

Shepherd 1: Well stay awake. We get to sleep later when the others wake up.

Shepherd 2: Okay, I'll try.

Narrator: Suddenly the shepherds heard a great noise. The sky began to grow bright.

Shepherd 1: Hey, what's happening?

Shepherd 2: I don't know, but I think everyone should see this.

(The two shepherds shake the others awake. Lead Angel enters and stands on the edge of platform, stage right.)

Shepherd 3: Where did she come from?

Shepherd 4: Maybe she's after our sheep.

Shepherd 5: She doesn't look like anyone I know.

(As the Shepherds talk, the Angel Choir enters and stands across the platform.)

Shepherd 1: Look, she brought friends.

Shepherd 2: I think we better get out of here.

(Shepherds stand up as if to run. Lead Angel steps forward and grabs one of the Shepherd's arms to stop him.)

Lead Angel: Please don't be scared. We're not going to hurt you.

Shepherd 3: Who are you?

Shepherd 4: Are you going to take our sheep?

Lead Angel: We didn't come here to take your sheep. We came to bring good news.

Shepherd 5: What good news?

Lead Angel: Unto you is born this day, in the city of David, a Savior, which is Christ the Lord.

Angel 2: And this shall be a sign unto you. You shall find the babe wrapped in swaddling clothes and lying in a manger.

Angel 3: See. It's good news.

Angel 4: Tell all your friends.

Angel Choir: Glory to God in the highest. Peace on Earth, good will toward men.

(As the Angels begin to exit, we notice that David had awakened and watched the whole thing.)

Shepherd 1: I want to see this baby.

Shepherd 2: Me, too.

Shepherd 3: Come on. Let's go to Bethlehem.

(Shepherds exit stage right. David gets up and watches Shepherds go.)

David: Wow! What was that? A Savior? A baby in Bethlehem? Hey, could that have been where King Melchior was going? I think I better follow those shepherds.

(David picks up bundle and blanket and runs off stage right after Shepherds. While he is exiting, Mary and Joseph enter stage left with Baby Jesus. They sit on platform center stage. Three Kings follow them in. They kneel on floor, their gifts in front of them. Esther kneels slightly behind King Melchior.)

King Caspar: Holy child, we have brought you gifts from our country. *(stands)* I have brought you gold.

(Caspar places gold at the feet of Mary and Joseph, then moves away standing stage left.)

King Balthazar: *(standing)* I have brought you sweet frankincense.

(Balthazar places gift and moves away stage right.)

King Melchior: *(standing)* Holy child, here is my gift, myrrh.

(The Shepherds enter in a hurry, grouping themselves around the Kings. David races in a little behind.)

David: Wait, please, let me give the gift!

King Melchior: But you didn't want to carry it. I believe you called it "dumb."

Esther: *(cringing)* Sorry, I had to tell him why you wouldn't come.

David: It's all right, Esther. King Melchior, I was the stupid one. I didn't understand. But, just before, I saw a miracle. I saw angels come down from heaven and speak of a holy child, and I understood why we made the trip.

King Melchior: That's very good. But it's too bad you needed proof.

David: Don't most people need proof?

Mary: There are some things God wants us to accept even without proof. The Baby Jesus was promised to us many years ago.

David: Nobody told me.

King Melchior: I tried to tell you. You wouldn't listen.

Joseph: God asks us to believe some things on faith.

Esther: King Melchior says faith is believing something *without* proof, just because God said so.

King Melchior: And we know God said so because it was written down in the ancient prophecies.

David: What's a prophecy?

King Balthazar: A promise for the future.

David: And this is one of God's promises?

Joseph: Made long ago. A Savior will come to bring us out of the darkness and into God's light.

David: *(to King Melchior)* Please, may I give the myrrh?

King Melchior: Yes, I think you should.

(David places the myrrh at the baby's feet. He stares down at the baby.)

David: He's ... perfect.

King Balthazar: A very true statement.

Esther: Aren't you glad you came now?

David: Yes. I'm sorry I didn't believe.

King Caspar: I think we should thank God for keeping his promises.

David: Thank you, God. Any other promises I should know? I'm ready to believe now.

King Melchior: We have a long journey back. That's gives us a lot of time to talk.

Narrator: David returned with the Kings back to his land, and he learned all about the ancient prophecies. As he grew up, his faith grew stronger. He became an able student of God's Word, and he never again doubted God's power and love. We all get like David sometimes and feel we can believe only what we can see. Faith is a muscle. It has to be exercised or it gets weak. In those times we have to cling tight to God's promises, and ask him to help us to believe. When we can do that, all God's promises become ours.
Jesus was born. Jesus lives. Amen.

Rehearsal For Christmas Eve

Characters (in order of appearance)

Director	Lead Angel
Stage Manager	Angel Choir
Youth Choir	Mary
Clark	Shepherd 2
Narrator	Shepherd 3
Shepherds	King 1
Angels	King 2
Lead Shepherd	King 3
Young Shepherd	

Props

Clipboards with paper
Script
Doll
Manger
Gifts for Baby Jesus from Wise Men

Notes

This is a "play within a play," which tells the story of one youthful actor's search for the real meaning of Christmas, and how he finds it at a Christmas pageant rehearsal. Because it is set in a church auditorium at an early rehearsal, the play requires no set, and only minimal costumes and props. It offers a range of roles for adults and teens, as well as children.

Musical interludes are inserted throughout the play, and particular carols are suggested for each one. These were the songs used in the original production. Other songs can be substituted, or, if preferred, these interludes can be removed. In the original production, the songs were performed by a chorus of Sunday school children, but they can be sung by solo voices, or even by the congregation as a whole.

(As the program begins, the Director and the Stage Manager are at the front of the auditorium holding clipboards and reviewing notes. A Youth Choir of all ages stands off left by a piano, singing. Other children stand off left and off right, or sit in front pews.)

Stage Manager: We've cast every part now but Joseph.

Director: I know. None of the boys want to play that part. I guess it's not as much fun as being a shepherd or a king. He doesn't have many lines. And he has to walk with a girl. You know how much the younger boys like that! *(thinks a bit)* Hey, how about Clark?

Stage Manager: Are you kidding? The last time I asked him to do something for the talent show, he told me, and I quote, "Only the dumb and the desperate perform in churches." Besides, he hardly ever comes to services. I don't think we could count on him to show up.

Director: You're right. It's a bad idea. Well, we'd better get started. I don't want to keep the little ones waiting too long.

(Director and Stage Manager lead out a group of little children, dressed as both Shepherds and Angels. The children stand in front of the platform. Director sits on the left side of first pew to watch the action. The Stage Manager stands left of children.)

Children: *(in unison)* "Joy, Joy, Joy
    God sent a Baby Boy
    To show us all His love
    He gave us Jesus from above"

Stage Manager: *(with children)* Welcome to our play!

(Children scurry off, Shepherds to the left, Angels to the right. Narrator enters from right and goes up on platform, holding a script. Clark, the boy talked about earlier, follows the Narrator out and sits in the first pew on the right side.)

Director: Don't you have that memorized yet?

Narrator: Unhh ... I forgot to take my script home last week. Look, I promise I'll have it memorized before the show.

Director: I hope so. Go ahead.

Narrator: *(reading much too rapidly)* Our story opens in a small field in which shepherds were looking after their flocks.

Director: Slow down!

Narrator: Sorry. *(slowing down to a normal speaking pace)* They had built a small fire and were huddled around it for warmth.

Stage Manager: Shepherds, that's your cue. *(Stage Manager brings the shepherds in from stage left and seats them in the center. One little child hangs back. Stage Manager gestures to child)* You, too.

Young Shepherd: No. I don't want to.

Director: That's all right. Come sit by me.

(Child runs over and sits next to Director.)

Director: You'll do it for the show, right?

Young Shepherd: *(shyly)* Sure, I think.

(Director hugs child.)

Narrator: The shepherds sang to themselves to keep awake.

(Shepherds sing "Away In A Manger" along with the Youth Choir off left.)

Narrator: Then suddenly the shepherds were startled by the appearance of an angel.

(Stage Manager steers Lead Angel from stage right to platform.)

Narrator: And the angel said ...

Lead Angel: *(nervously)* Uh ...

Narrator: *(annoyed)* And the angel said ...

Stage Manager: *(cueing her)* "For unto you is born ..."

Lead Angel: Oh yeah ... For unto you is born *(begins to speak faster and faster)* in the city of David a Savior, which is Christ the Lord. And this shall be a sign unto you. You shall find the babe wrapped in swaddling clothes and lying in a manger.

Director: *(applauding)* I'm really impressed.

Lead Angel: *(with a smug look at Narrator)* I've been practicing every day.

(Narrator returns snotty glance to Lead Angel as Stage Manager leads the Angel Choir from stage right up to platform.)

Narrator: Then suddenly there was with the angels a multitude of the heavenly host, praising God and saying ...

Angel Choir: Glory to God in the highest. Peace on Earth. Good will to men.

(All Angels and Youth Choir sing one verse of "Hark! The Herald Angels Sing," before exiting off right with Stage Manager's help.)

Lead Shepherd: *(standing up)* Let's go to Bethlehem and see this miracle that God has made.

(Shepherds all stand and move off left. At the same time, Clark stands up and faces the director.)

Clark: What does it mean? You do this every year. Why do you bother?

Director: You really want to know? Take a part and maybe you'll find out.

Clark: No, thanks. *(stands up and begins walking up center aisle)*

Stage Manager: *(calling out)* Why not?

Clark: I don't like this kind of stuff.

Director: So why are you here?

Clark: *(turning around)* I had nothing else to do.

Director: Okay, since you have nothing else to do, why don't you read the part of Joseph?

Clark: No, I don't like plays!

Stage Manager: *(walking to the boy)* It would be a big help to the others if you'd just read the part to help them rehearse. And since you don't have anything to do ...

Clark: Well ...

Director: Please?

Clark: Okay. But just for today.

Stage Manager: Terrific! I'll show you where you enter.

(Stage Manager leads Clark up center aisle to the back and hands him a script. Mary is already there and eyes her Joseph warily.)

Director: Mary and Joseph, come on in.

(Mary and Joseph come up center aisle. Mary is holding Jesus and is very wrapped up in what she's doing. Clark follows behind. Mary sets down manger and sits on floor in front of platform. Joseph, after hesitating, follows suit.)

Clark: *(loud whisper to Mary)* Do I say anything?

Mary: Not now. Just sing.

Clark: *(fumbling with script)* Sing what?

Mary: Just listen. You'll learn.

(Shepherds reenter, standing left and right of Mary and Joseph. All sing "What Child Is This?" After the song is finished, the Shepherds exit off left.)

Narrator: The shepherds weren't the only visitors who came to worship our Savior.

Clark: *(to Mary)* What's "Savior" mean?

Mary: *(answering out of the corner of her mouth)* It means Jesus came to save us.

Clark: *(a bit louder)* From what?

Mary: Our sins. You know, all the bad stuff we do.

Clark: *(louder still)* A little baby did that?

(Mary looks at Joseph and replies very sincerely.)

Mary: This wasn't just "any little baby."

(Narrator gives an annoyed look at the whispering.)

Narrator: Can I finish?

Director: Relax. That dialogue was more important. *(smiles at Narrator)* Okay, continue ...

Narrator: Some Kings from a far-off land, who had been studying the sky, noticed an unusually bright star had appeared on the horizon. They knew from old prophecy ... What did you say that meant?

Director: Predicting the future. Knowing something before it happens. And say "ancient prophecy," not "old prophecy."

Narrator: *(nods)* They knew from ancient prophecy that the star could signify the birth of a new king. And so they set out to find him. They followed the star all the way to Bethlehem.

(Kings come down center aisle, each carrying a small package. All sing "We Three Kings.")

Clark: *(points to Baby Jesus)* These guys came a long distance to see him?

Mary: Yes, I told you, he was a *special* baby.

Narrator: They brought him gifts.

(Kings stand in a single file in front of Mary and Joseph. As each says their line, they place a gift in front of the baby and then move to stand on either side of the couple.)

King 1: I brought gold.

King 2: I brought sweet frankincense.

King 3: And I brought costly myrrh.

Mary: *(to Clark)* That's why we give each other Christmas presents. Because the Kings gave presents to Jesus.

(Director stands and walks to Clark.)

Director: And even more importantly, because God gave us the greatest gift of all at Christmas. His own Son, Jesus.

Clark: What kind of gift was that?

Narrator: A gift of life, love, and happiness. God's Son came to remove our sins, so one day we could be with God.

Clark: I'm not sure, but I think I'm starting to understand. Could I ... would it be too late to do this part for real?

Director: I think you'll do just fine.

(Stage Manager and Director bring all children out center. Everyone sings "Silent Night.")

All: Merry Christmas!

Clark: A very Merry Christmas.

Journey To The Heart Of Christmas

Characters (in order of appearance)

Narrator	Gloria
Miriam	Mary
Hamid	Joseph
David	Mark
Aaron	Jordana
Joy	Ruth
Harmony	Faith

Props

Name tags
Lectern
Chairs
Logs, piled up to simulate a fire
Large, fancy bottle
Tied-up bundle filled with clothes and a blanket
Small notebook
Pen/pencil
Three pairs of dark sunglasses
Dish cloth
Apron
Blanket
Soup pot and two bowls
Loaf of bread
Telescope

Notes

"Journey To The Heart Of Christmas" speculates on stories of the youngest witnesses to Christ's birth. It offers a mix of speaking roles, from basic one or two line parts for the littlest ones, to more substantial roles for older youth. The Angels should have name tags large enough that the audience can read their names.

Stage will be bare throughout most of the play, except for a lectern and chair for the Narrator upstage right, a chair placed just off stage right, and a group of logs piled up downstage right to simulate a fire.

———————

Narrator: Year after year, we retell the story of Christ's miraculous birth. Most of us can recite the reaction of all the key players ... the Shepherds' fear, the Angels' joy, the quiet happiness of Mary and Joseph, the reverence of the visiting Kings. Legends have even celebrated how the animals each made their contribution to the baby king.

(Miriam, a young Jewish girl whose parents are traveling merchants enters from the stage right aisle, while Hamid, the young apprentice to a wise King from the East enters from the stage left aisle. Hamid is carrying a large fancy looking bottle. Miriam holds a tied-up bundle filled with clothes. The two should reach the edge of the stage just about the same time as the Narrator finishes. One will stay on the left side of the stage and the other on the right. All the other "witnesses" will pass one of these children, but the two of them will not meet until the end of the play.)

Narrator: What we never read about is how the young children of the time might have felt. What did they see? How did they react? Today, we are going to use God's gift of imagination to show the different ways the children of Bethlehem welcomed the newborn king. We're mainly going to tell this through two witnesses, Miriam, a young Jewish girl whose parents were traveling merchants, going from town to town to sell silks, spices, and farming tools; and Hamid, a young apprentice to a King from the East, who carries a very special gift for the newborn king. Let's now go on the road with Hamid and Miriam who are both headed to the "heart of Christmas."

Miriam: *(directly to the audience)* At last, I see Bethlehem. I can't believe how long it has taken us to get here. With that census thing, the roads are so crowded. Everyone is traveling back to the town of their birth to register. It's been great for my family. We have sold so many things, particularly jugs to carry water. Dad says if this keeps up, we may be able to head home to Nazareth and not have to work for months. But, boy, am I tired. I'm so glad we're finally making camp for the night. *(sits stage right, opens up her bundle, sets a blanket down, and pretends to warm herself by a fire)*

Hamid: *(pulling out a small notebook and pretending to write in it)* Journal entry number one. We left in such a hurry, I had no time to record the information about this trip. Sometime ago, my master came to me all excited. He told me to pack enough of his things for a long journey, one that could last as long as two years. We've never traveled that far on one of these journeys. Then, he asked me to take a pitcher of his precious frankincense. Now, normally, we don't take along the frankincense unless we're visiting someone important. I mean, you don't bring along frankincense when you drop in on the local telescope salesman. And, though my master always knows where he's going, this time, he said he really didn't know our destination. We were going to follow this STAR he had been watching. Now chasing after a star doesn't seem very wise to me, but he said this particular star had been foretold centuries ago, and that when the star stopped, we would find a new king who would set the world free. We have been on the road for quite some time now, but something tells me we've still got a long way to go. But, not today. My feet are killing me. *(sits stage left, puts down the jug of frankincense, then rubs his feet)*

Narrator: Hamid still had miles to go. He watched the night sky, looking for this special star his master said they were following. But, he just saw the usual field of stars twinkling in the dark. As he was watching, he thought he saw something far in the distance, a star that seemed just a little bit bigger, a little brighter than the others. He drifted off to sleep, watching this star twinkle and glow in the distance. Far, far away, Miriam saw the sky grow very bright. Then, out of the brightness, she saw two boys rushing toward her. They were dressed as shepherds. Miriam thought it very strange that two children should be running around alone so late at night. She stood up and called to them.

(David and Aaron run in from stage right and run slightly past Miriam. They turn around and come back to her when she calls out.)

Miriam: Hello, shepherd boys. What are you doing out here by yourselves?

David: We're looking for the baby angel. Have you seen her?

Miriam: Baby, what?

Aaron: The baby angel. We saw her for just one minute and then she disappeared.

Miriam: Baby angel? You guys must be seeing things. I've traveled these roads all my life. I've never seen an angel. Maybe it was a bird or something. Come over here by the fire and get warm and tell me what you think you saw. And why are you out here all by yourself, anyway?

David: Tonight, our father asked us if we'd like to come to the fields with him.

Aaron: He usually doesn't like us to come, but he said the flock was so large right now, he needed our help.

David: I was a little scared of the dark.

Aaron: That's because you're not used to it. I've gone out with Dad more than you. It didn't bother me ... much!

David: Anyway, I sat there watching the stars when I saw something. Like a light ... not a big flash of light. Something small and gentle.

Aaron: We looked a little closer and then we saw ... an angel.

Miriam: Yeah, right. And the next thing you're going to tell me is that she had some special message, just for you. I've heard about you shepherds and the weird things you think when you're out alone in the fields.

Aaron: We're not making this up. I swear on my daddy's flock.

David: And we never, ever swear on our daddy's flock. It's too important.

(Very quietly, Joy, a little angel enters from stage left.)

Miriam: Well, I haven't seen any angels. And, you should go back to your father. *(picks up a log and dips into the fire, making a torch)* Here, this will help you find your way. Be careful, you don't want to trip over that little angel ... angel? *(to Joy)* What are you doing here?

Joy: I'm lost.

Miriam: I'll say. Heaven is only about 1,000 miles that way. *(points up)*

David: See, we told you it was an angel ... and look, there's another one.

(Harmony, a slightly older angel, enters from stage left.)

Harmony: Joy. Come back. We've been looking all over for you.

(Joy runs to Harmony.)

Joy: I was lost.

Harmony: I told you to stay with us. Why are you always looking at those stars?

David: It's an angel invasion.

(Gloria, a still older angel, enters from left with Faith, another small angel, and takes the two girls by the hand.)

Gloria: Not an invasion, an invitation, which we've come to deliver to you personally. We were going to share it with all the shepherds, but since Joy decided to get a better look at the stars over here, I guess we'll tell you and you can share it with the others. *(calls up)* Could we have a little light here? *(to the children)* You might want to shield your eyes ... or better yet, put on these. *(hands them dark sunglasses)*

Aaron: What are these things?

Gloria: They're called sunglasses. Trust me, they're going to be very popular in the future.

Faith: Is it time to sing now?

Gloria: Yes, Faith, it's time to sing. Are you ready?

All Angels: YES!

Narrator: Suddenly the sky grew very, very bright. To the children, it was like the sun had suddenly burst into the night sky, only ten times brighter. Through the "sunglasses" the angels gave them, they saw not just the three angels, but a whole sky full of angels. The children were very afraid, but the older angel, Gloria told them:

Gloria: Fear not. For behold I bring you tidings of great joy which shall be to all people. Unto you is born this day, in the city of David *(points to the left),* that place over there, a Savior which is Christ the Lord. And, this shall be a sign unto you, you shall find the baby, wrapped in swaddling clothes and lying in a manger. *(to the other angels)* Okay, big finish ...

All Angels: Glory to God in the highest. And peace and good will to all.

Gloria: Well, don't just stand there. Spread the word. Tell everyone. And if they don't believe, keep telling them. A miracle is happening *(points to left)* that way.

Faith: Did we do okay?

Gloria: You did fine. Now we need to get you all home.

(Angels and Shepherds exit off right. One of the Angels moves the chair up to stage right. Another takes away the logs.)

Narrator: And, just like that, the angels disappeared, taking those sunglass things with them. Miriam sent the shepherd boys back to their father, who she could hear calling out to them. Then she went to tell her parents what she had heard. Of course, they didn't believe her. After all, she was just a child. So, after they fell asleep, Miriam slipped away and headed for Bethlehem. *(Miriam picks up blanket and bundle, then exits stage right.)* While the bright light had gone with the angels, the stars were unusually bright. And, there was one star that seemed to be moving, lighting her way. Meanwhile, far, far away, Hamid was noticing that same star. He was now sure this was the star his master had spoken about.

Hamid: Journal entry number two. I've spent all night tracking the star and it's definitely moving. I woke up the master and said we should move now or we might lose it. But he said, "Patience. The star will guide us in good time. We still have many miles to go. Get some rest." But, who can sleep? I pulled out one of the master's scrolls, the one that he says told him to follow the star. I don't read all that well, but I just have a feeling the King it says is coming has arrived tonight.

(Mary and Joseph enter from the back of the sanctuary. They walk up the aisle as Hamid talks. When he finishes, they sit down center stage. Jordana, a kitchen servant enters, and sits stage right. She

85

has a dishcloth over one shoulder and she rubs the other. Hamid leaves the stage, but remains in view, stage left.)

Narrator: Hamid was right, the King had come and Mary and Joseph were just putting him to bed. It wasn't much of a bed, just the feedbox where the animals ate hay. But after walking all day, Mary and Joseph were grateful for warm and dry shelter. It had been a busy day at the inn. Everyone from the innkeeper's children to the young servant girls who worked in the kitchen had not stopped for a moment, as meals needed to be prepared, and beds made for the visitors coming from far and wide for the census the Emperor had ordered.

Jordana: *(calling off right)* Ruth. Enough already. Take a break. It's so much cooler out here.

Ruth: *(entering from right, wiping her hands on an apron)* Take a break? We have a sink full of dirty dishes yet, and the master's wife just asked me to warm up the leftover soup.

Jordana: It can wait two minutes. I've been cleaning pots since early this morning. My shoulders feel like a camel sat on them. The inn is full. No one else is arriving tonight. I just want to sit for two minutes and feel a cool breeze on my face.

Ruth: Okay, two minutes. But no more. I don't ever remember a day like this. If I let that soup boil over the missus will take it out of my wages, and I can't afford to lose any money.

Jordana: I can just hear the money dropping in the master's coin box. He's getting rich and we're getting dishpan hands. What do they need the soup for? I thought everyone had gone to bed.

Ruth: You didn't hear? Two travelers arrived just a little while ago, a man and his wife, and the woman was about to give birth. The soup is for them. They looked so hungry and tired that the missus ordered me to get them something to eat and make them as comfortable as possible.

Jordana: But, there are no rooms left. Where did he put them?

Ruth: *(laughing)* The stable. Can you imagine? Her giving birth with all those animals and everything?

Jordana: Boy, the master will do anything to make money, won't he?

Ruth: Actually, I think the boss felt sorry for them.

Jordana: Hey, let's go have a look.

Ruth: Sure, but let me get the soup and some bread to take out to them.

(Ruth and Jordana exit off right as the Shepherds reenter from right. Mark, the stable boy, enters from left and stands in front of Mary and Joseph.)

Narrator: As Ruth and Jordana prepared the food, the Shepherds arrived. Mark, the stable boy, who had been surprised to find Mary and Joseph in the barn, didn't want to let the shepherds in.

Mark: My boss doesn't let strangers in the barn. It scares the cows.

David: But the angels sent us.

Aaron: We ran all the way here. Our father and the others are coming, too. We want to see the Baby King.

Joseph: Please, let them in. I don't think your boss will mind. This is ... kind of a special event.

Mark: Okay, but try not to wake up the cows.

(Shepherds kneel by the baby as Miriam comes running in, followed by Jordana and Ruth. Jordana holds a blanket and a loaf of bread, while Ruth carries a large pot of soup and two bowls.)

Mary: Wow! What a welcome. Thanks, all of you.

Ruth: We brought you some soup and bread, and a blanket for the baby.

Mary: It is a little chilly. Why don't you cover him with it?

Miriam: What's his name?

Mary: Jesus.

Jordana: That's a strange name. Why not John or Adam?

David: Or, David, like me?

Joseph: It's kind of a long story. This is a baby born for a special purpose. So, he sort of needs a special name. Besides, there already was a famous David in my family. I don't think we need another one.

Ruth: Special purpose? How can he have a purpose when he can't even talk yet?

Mary: Not all purposes require talking. I don't know exactly how, but God told me his life is going to change the world.

Miriam: But, he's just a baby!

Joseph: Well, it's not going to happen overnight. Though, in some ways, I guess he has changed the world overnight ... this night ... just by coming here.

Aaron: I'm confused.

Mary: I promise. It will all make sense in time. But, right now, I have a very special purpose for all of you.

Joseph: You need to tell others that the Prince of Peace has come.

Jordana: Can I finish the pots first?

Mary: Yes, it can wait until after the kitchen is clean. Now, if you don't mind, I think the baby needs to sleep.

Mark: That's right. Everybody out of my barn. Let the baby sleep.

Miriam: But the others ... my parents, the other shepherds ... they're all coming.

Joseph: Well, if your parents are meeting you here, maybe you could stay outside and tell anyone who comes to enter very quietly.

(All children will step offstage and sit on the floor below center stage. When the Narrator says, "they returned ..." all will exit down side and back aisles. Hamid will reenter stage left and will move to center stage.)

Narrator: And so all the children camped outside the stable, keeping watch and telling all to enter quietly. In the morning, they returned to their flocks and their jobs in the kitchen, and Miriam and her family returned to their travels. Hamid and the Kings continued their journey as well.

Hamid: Journal entry number 121. The star continues to move and continues to shine brighter than all the others. It doesn't seem to matter whether the sky is clear or cloudy. It still shines through. We continue to track it. Some of the servants, and even one of the Kings, have begun to doubt we'll ever reach our destination. One even suggested that we're moving to the edge of the world and will then fall off it into space. I have not lost faith, and I think we are now almost there. The shepherds we have met on our journey have told us of a miraculous birth occurring in Bethlehem. My master is sure this is the infant king we seek, but the shepherds said he is no longer there. That he and his family have gone home. I miss *my* home. I've lost track of time and don't know how long it's been, but I'm tired of sleeping on the ground. Please, Star of Wonder, show us where he is now. *(pulls out a telescope and looks up)*

Narrator: Right on cue, the star paused and grew even brighter. Hamid was ready to run to tell his master, when he saw a group of travelers approaching. It was Miriam and her family. Our two wanderers, who had been tracking the star for so long, were finally going to meet.

(Miriam will reenter from the center aisle. She is carrying her bundle again and is tired after walking all day. She will go up on the stage, at right, where she began the play.)

Miriam: *(calling off to her parents)* This looks like a good spot to camp. It's right near the crossroads, so we can enter Nazareth early tomorrow. I'm going to build the fire right there, where those camels are. Who can afford to travel with camels?

Hamid: A King can.

Miriam: *(startled, she turns around quickly and sees Hamid)* Who are you ... and who are they? *(pointing off to the Kings)*

Hamid: Don't be afraid. I work for a very wise King. We've traveled a great distance and our supplies are running low. Might you have some water for our camels? And maybe something to eat?

Miriam: *(curtsying)* We're only poor merchants at the end of a long trip. We don't have much left, but whatever we have is yours.

Hamid: Anything you may have is fine. And thanks for your kindness. We are in a bit of a hurry, though. See, the star has stopped and we are anxious to complete our journey.

Miriam: Which star? Is it that big bright one that's been in the eastern sky since the baby was born?

90

Hamid: *(excitedly)* You know about the baby? Tell us, where is he now?

Miriam: Well, I don't really know. I got to see him the night he was born. But that was back in Bethlehem. His parents were only there for the census. I'm sure they've gone back to their home by now.

Hamid: Please, you must know. My master has been waiting for years to find the one the prophets called the King of kings, the one who would save us from our sins, and bring the world out of darkness.

Miriam: *(to herself)* That must be the "special purpose" Mary talked about. And, I guess it's time to do my job. *(to Hamid)* The town down there is my hometown, Nazareth. And if the star has stopped, he must be there. Come, I will lead you and your King down there. *(yelling off to parents)* Mom, Dad, forget the camp. We have to lead some Kings into Nazareth.

(Miriam and Hamid both run off left. As the Narrator reads, all the children will reenter and go up on the stage. Hamid and Miriam should enter last. Music can play under the narration.)

Narrator: So, because Miriam remembered the job Joseph and Mary had given her, and Hamid had remained faithful to the promises of the prophets, and the shepherds had listened and acted on the words of the angels, Christ's work on Earth — his purpose — could begin. Each of these young people saw the birth in a different way, but the message behind the gift — the gift tag — reads the same to all men, women, and children, kitchen worker or stable boy, merchant's child or king. God so loved the world that he gave us the best, most personal gift of all ... his own Son. All for us. Thank you, Lord, and Merry Christmas.

No Small Parts

Characters (in order of appearance)

First Child (Lead Angel)   Mother (offstage voice)
Second Child (Lead Shepherd) Costumer
Third Child (Mary)   Stage Manager
Fourth Child (Second Angel)   Narrator
Fifth Child (Third Angel)   Second Shepherd
Joseph   Third Shepherd
Director (Mrs. Cassidy)   Angel Choir
"Real" Joseph (RJ)

Props

Scripts
Robe
Angel costume parts
Sewing accessories

Notes

This is another play that would work well with multigenerational casting. The Director, the "Real" Joseph, the Stage Manager, and the Costumer can all be played by adults or teens. The lead part of Joseph was written with a 'tween in mind — a child somewhere between ten and twelve. The balance of the parts are short enough for younger elementary children. If you have a large group of children, you can have an endless number of angels and shepherds, and can even add some single-line parts.

The setting is a church auditorium, several weeks before Christmas. Children are gathering for a rehearsal of the annual Christmas play.

(As the play opens, a group of children enter from stage right, clutching scripts. They have just been assigned their parts for the play and all are very happy, except for the young actor who has been cast as Joseph. He slinks in a minute or two after the others.)

First Child: Lead Angel. All right! Look at this great speech I get to give. And, I heard the director say they're going to have a spotlight on me when I talk.

Second Child: I've got a long speech, too.

First Child: *(breaking in)* It's called a monologue.

Second Child: Yeah, whatever. And *(counting)*, 1-2-3-4-5-6 other lines, too. This is the biggest part I've ever had.

Third Child: It doesn't matter how many lines you have. Everyone will be looking at me, Mary, in my beautiful blue and white costume.

Fourth Child: Well, I think my angel costume is prettier, and when that spotlight hits it ...

Third Child: But, Mary is the *star*!

Fifth Child: Mrs. Cassidy says there are no stars — that all our parts are important.

First Child: *(shaking his/her head, talking with the "voice of experience")* Don't you know she only says that so the children without lines don't feel bad? Trust me. There are stars. And, I'm one of them.

Second Child: Well, I may not be a star. But at least I get to say something. Not like Joseph.

Fourth Child: Yeah. He doesn't get to say anything. He just stands there and *(making a concerned face)* looks concerned. *(all giggle)*

Joseph: I'm glad someone finds this funny. I sure don't. It's not fair. I played Joseph last year. One time is all right, but twice in a row?

First Child: *(shrugging)* Maybe the director doesn't think you can remember a lot of lines.

Fourth Child: Maybe she just doesn't think you're a good actor.

Joseph: But I am and she knows it. I had the lead in the school play last spring and she was in the audience. She even told me I was good.

(The Director enters from stage right just in time to hear what the Fourth Child said.)

Director: Yes, I told him he was good, and I meant it. It's because he is such a good actor that I gave him the part. Sometimes the parts without words are the toughest ones to play. You act with more than just your mouth, you know. Joseph wasn't a man of words. The Bible doesn't quote him. But he had a good heart and, more important, he was ready to do whatever God asked of him. Joseph spoke with his actions, kind of like Vin Diesel minus the guns.

Joseph: I'm not on stage long enough to do any actions. Look, give me something a little bigger, one of the kings or even a shepherd, and I'll show you some great acting — with or without guns.

Director: But I really need you as Joseph. No one else can do this part. Hey, there's an old saying in the theater that goes: "There are no small parts, only small actors."

Joseph: And what's that supposed to mean?

Director: Think about it. *(crosses front toward main doors, then turns around and faces everyone)* Why don't you all think about that? *(exits)*

Joseph: *(asking Third Child)* What do you think it means?

Third Child: *(thinks for a minute, then shrugs)* I don't know. Maybe there's a lot of short actors around. Don't worry about it. I think you'll make a great Joseph.

Fourth Child: Why not? You've already done it once.

First Child: Well, I'm going home to learn my lines. Want to come back to my house? We could rehearse together.

Second Child: Great idea. Let me just call my mom.

Fifth Child: *(to Joseph)* Are you coming?

Joseph: Why? I don't think I need to rehearse *(mimicking Fourth Child)* standing and looking concerned.

Fourth Child: Look, I'm sorry about that. I didn't mean it.

Joseph: It's okay. You guys go ahead, I'm gonna hang around a while.

Fifth Child: See you at rehearsal.

(All children exit through main doors, then reenter to side room. Joseph sits down and stares at the script. He climbs onto stage and crosses his arm, trying several different ways of "looking concerned." Disgusted, he drops the script and sits on the edge of the stage.)

Joseph: Well, I don't care what anyone says. There are small parts and this is the smallest. Even Vin Diesel couldn't make this look big. This guy's a loser. He never talks and he doesn't do anything. Mary does all the work.

(From stage left, the "Real" Joseph appears and sits on the other side of the platform.)

"Real" Joseph (RJ): I know what you mean. I felt the same way. And I had to live through it.

(Joseph had not seen the "Real" Joseph enter and now he jumps back in surprise.)

Joseph: Who are you? And where did you come from?

RJ: I'm sorry I startled you. And I apologize for not introducing myself. *(extends a hand)* My name is Joseph, well, Joseph of Nazareth, to be precise. You're playing me.

Joseph: *(panicky)* Look, my mom will be here any minute now, and the pastor is just down the hall in his study. He'd be in here in a minute if I scream, so why don't you just go?

RJ: Hey, I mean you no harm. I wouldn't harm anyone. I'm a loser who never does anything, remember?

Joseph: So, what are you? A ghost or something? Have you come to haunt me?

RJ: No, nothing like that. I'm just here for a few minutes to help you think.

Joseph: Listen — you can tell whoever set you up to do this that I don't like playing ... you. And no actor in a ratty bathrobe is going to change my mind.

RJ: *(pulling at his robe)* Well, I'll admit it's no Tommy Hilfiger, but it was fashionable for the time. Look, nobody "set you up," and I'm not here to confuse you. I just wanted to help you do what your director said. Think about this part and how important it really was.

Joseph: *(picking up the script and showing it to RJ)* It's small.

RJ: Only in words.

Joseph: Well what else is there? The Bible stories are all we have to tell us about that night, and you're barely even mentioned. If you were so important, why isn't more written about you?

RJ: Well, no written account, even one inspired by God, can tell the whole story. Hey, look. I asked all these kinds of questions, too. God asked me to take an awful big leap of faith in doing what I did, and don't think I didn't have my doubts. There was a point when I wasn't even sure I wanted anything to do with Mary, or with God's plans for Baby Jesus. But, God talked to me and he let me see just where I fit in. I had a really important job to do, even if it wasn't as flashy as singing in the sky or following a star.

Joseph: *(sarcastically)* Then just what did you do?

RJ: Think about it. Who watched over Mary and got her safely to Bethlehem? Who led the donkey? Who found the inn and persuaded the innkeeper to let us stay in the stable? And, later, when King Herod threatened to kill Jesus, who saw that he made it to Egypt where he'd be safe? I'm not boasting, but if it hadn't been for me, things might not have worked out. And, let's not forget that it was through me that God allowed the prophecy to be fulfilled — that a Savior would come from the family of David.

Joseph: *(genuinely impressed)* You really were kind of a Vin Diesel, weren't you?

RJ: I prefer Schwarzenegger myself. Better hairline.

Joseph: So why don't you ever get lines in the pageant? Why don't we see you doing all this cool stuff?

RJ: I'm afraid that what I did didn't seem very special at the time. I was just being a good husband and father, like a lot of other men at the time. But, that's okay. I wasn't doing this for glory. I was doing it for Mary and my son. And I was doing it because it was the role God wanted me to play in this story. Just like you could be doing in this play.

Joseph: I get it. It's not about how long you're on stage, or how many lines you say, or even if the audience notices you. It's about doing what we can, as best as we can, so the story gets told.

RJ: Right. There's a part for all of us in God's plan. All we can do is play it the best we can.

Joseph: I will. *(shakes "Real" Joseph's hand)* and thank you. Boy, wait 'til I tell the other kids about you.

RJ: Don't try to tell them. They'll just think you're crazy. Show them. God can still work miracles, but he doesn't want us to expect them. He hopes we'll take things on faith. So, don't mention my visit, okay?

Joseph: *(reluctantly)* Okay. Thanks.

RJ: You'll do fine. *(gets up and starts to exit stage left, then turns back to Joseph)* And, do me one favor? Not that I'm vain, or anything, but don't wear that ratty beard this year. Give me some dignity, okay?

Joseph: *(laughing)* That thing is pretty ratty. Okay, you got it. No beard.

RJ: Take care.

("Real" Joseph exits stage left. Joseph watches him go, shaking his head in amazement.)

Mother: *(offstage)* Are you coming? I've been waiting here, and your brother needs a diaper change.

Joseph: I'm coming. I was just getting some special stage directions.

(Joseph exits through center door. After a brief pause, all the children come milling in from stage right. Some are in costume, others just in pieces of costumes. Costumer is busy working on one of the Angel costumes. The Director enters from center doors off right, followed by the Stage Manager.)

Director: Okay, let's get started. Everybody get where you belong. We're going to start with the Angel scene, and that means I need Shepherds down front. Angels, you get up on the platform. Big Angels, help the little angels.

(All move to do as the Director said. Fourth Child starts to move on stage with Costumer still stitching pieces together.)

Costumer: Look, if you want to have costumes for this thing, I need to try stuff on and make alterations. There's a bunch of kids whose measurements I didn't even get yet.

Director: Not now. The kids have to rehearse.

Costumer: Well, unless you want a bunch of naked Angels up there....

Director: We'll knock off a few minutes early and you can do it then.

Costumer: All right. But nobody leaves without seeing me first.

(Costumer moves off to stage right. Stage Manager helps get the children into place. Director sits in front pew, right side. The Narrator goes up to the podium.)

Director: Start with the Lead Angel's speech.

Narrator: Can't I say my lines first?

Stage Manager: It would be easier if we started with the narration.

Director: You're right. Start from there.

Narrator: There were shepherds in the fields, watching their flocks. Suddenly, the sky lit up and a host of heavenly angels appeared. The shepherds were very frightened.

First Child (Lead Angel): Fear not, for behold I bring you good tidings of great joy. For unto you is born this day in the city of David, a ... How do you say the next word?

Director: A Savior ...

First Child (Lead Angel): Right ... a Savior, which is Christ the Lord. And this shall be a sign unto you. You shall find the baby wrapped in swaddling clothes, and lying in a manger.

Director: Okay, all the Angels together ...

Angel Choir: Glory to God in the highest. Peace on Earth, good will to men.

Fourth Child (Second Angel): Is that all we get to say?

Stage Manager: *(checks script)* Yeah, that's it.

Director: And you did it very well, too. Now, Angels, you go off right, and the Lead Shepherd will stay.

Fourth Child (Second Angel): *(interrupting)* But, my aunt is coming all the way from Brooklyn just to see me. Couldn't I say a little bit more? Like "Follow us, we'll lead you there"?

Fifth Child (Third Angel): The angels didn't lead them. A star did.

First Child (Lead Angel): No, a star lead the Kings ...

Fourth Child (Second Angel): How about, "Go on. We'll watch the sheep"?

Director: Sorry, the show is running long. But, I'll tell you what *(to Fourth Child)*, you can be in charge of all the baby angels, okay?

Fourth Child (Second Angel): *(shrugs)* Okay. *(to little ones)* Come on. Let's go.

(All Angels exit right.)

Second Child (Lead Shepherd): Let us go to Bethlehem and find this baby.

Second Shepherd: But we can't just leave the sheep.

Second Child (Lead Shepherd): The sheep will be fine. God will watch over them.

Third Shepherd: Let's hurry then. I want to see this baby for myself.

(Shepherds get up. Second Child appears to be ready to say some more, but the Stage Manager comes up to lead them down the center aisle.)

Second Child (Lead Shepherd): *(breaking character)* But wait. I haven't said my monologue yet, and I have two other lines after that.

Stage Manager: *(checks script)* Nope, you don't say anything else.

Director: I told everyone the play was running too long and we had to cut some lines. Didn't you check the revised script I gave you?

Second Child (Lead Shepherd): No ... I didn't think you were cutting any of my lines. I thought we were just dropping the dumb old Kings.

Director: No, we cut a little bit from everyone so we didn't have to cut out any parts.

First Child: So I guess it's down to just two lines, huh?

(Lead Shepherd walks off in a pout.)

Director: *(calling over her shoulder)* Mary and Joseph, this is where you come in.

Narrator: The shepherds ran to the stable to greet Baby Jesus.

(Mary peeks out from stage left.)

Mary (Third Child): I'm here, but Joseph isn't.

Director: Has anyone seen him?

Fourth Child: *(finally fully in her Angel costume)* He felt pretty bad about being Joseph again. Maybe he's not coming....

Director: But we really need him as Joseph. He's the only one in the group that can pull it off.

Stage Manager: Should I check to see who else we have?

(Joseph bursts through the double doors stage right. He's carrying bits of his costume with him.)

Joseph: *(slightly out of breath)* I'm sorry I'm late. I was working on my part.

Mary (Third Child): But what did you have to work on?

Joseph: Oh, there was a lot to figure out. I wanted to make sure I'd be the best Joseph ever.

Fourth Child: But you have no lines!

Joseph: Yeah, but I wanted to think about my costume, and how Joseph would have walked, and what he might have been thinking about, and what he'd be carrying.

Director: I'm glad to hear that. *(looking around)* Everyone should take his or her part that seriously. And you really don't mind playing Joseph?

Joseph: Mind? This is a great part. Maybe one of the most important in the play.

Director: *(smiling)* No small part, only small actors.

Joseph: Yeah. I figured out what you meant by that. Every part in a play is important. Take any character out, and the play loses something. Just like every person has a part to play in God's plan.

Third Child: Well, what does the part about small actors mean? *(looking at Joseph)* He doesn't look any smaller.

Joseph: It means ... I can't explain ...

Director: It means being so concerned about getting credit or attention, or having the most lines, that you don't do a good job with the part you have. Being too small up here *(points to her head)* to see how you fit in with the whole play. Understand?

All Children: Yes.

Director: Good. Now we can finish this rehearsal. *(looking at Joseph)* But, tell me, how did you figure all this out?

Joseph: I had a little help from someone who really understood how I felt.

Director: Oh, really? Who?

Joseph: A really old friend ... But nobody you'd know, at least not in person.

Director: I don't understand.

Joseph: Think about it.

The Greatest News Of All

Characters (in order of appearance)

Narrator

Bureau Chief

Reporter (Ace)

Shepherd 1

Shepherd 2

Shepherd 3

Shepherd 4

Other Shepherds (nonspeaking)

Angel 1

Angel 2

Angel 3

Angel Choir

Maid

Rachel

Innkeeper's Wife

Stable Boy

Mary

Joseph

Props

Desk

Chair

Phone

Fake computer

Notebook

Pencil

Cardboard door

Bowl

Spoon

Makeshift cradle

Doll

Bigger cradle

Notes

"The Greatest News Of All" is one of our "anachronism" plays, where we insert elements from the present — in this case an Internet News Bureau — into the world of Christ's birth to present a different twist on the Christmas story. It has a good number of speaking parts but, except for the Reporter and Bureau Chief, all are relatively short, making them easy roles for younger children.

The only fixed set pieces are a desk and chair downstage right. A phone and some facsimile of a computer should sit on the desk (you can make a pretty real-looking laptop out of a shoebox and some black spray paint). Some simple stage lighting should be used, if at all possible.

———————

(As the play starts, the Narrator moves up to the podium, which should be on the far right or far left of the stage so as not to block the action. If this is not possible, the Narrator should be positioned, with a handheld microphone just offstage.)

Narrator: It would be very hard to imagine a world without the news. Satellites and sophisticated equipment have made it possible for us to always know what's going on. If something happens on the other side of the world, we'll know about it only minutes later through radio, television, and especially, the internet.

But when the greatest news event of all time happened, there were no reporters to cover the story. No television cameras to put it on film. No blogs to debate its authenticity. The event was the birth of Jesus Christ, and the message of the "good news" was not broadcast over the radio, but instead was told and retold by angels and shepherds, and later, kings.

What would have happened if the technology had existed for reporters to be present at Jesus' birth? Did you ever wonder how that might have sounded on the radio? Or looked as a story on a website? Lend us your imagination for a few minutes while we take a look at what it might have been like.

(Bureau Chief enters and sits at a desk stage right.)

Narrator: We take you now to the Bethlehem Bureau of Middle Eastern News Services, the largest online news agency in the known world. The Bureau Chief, who ran the office, was tired. All day he had been getting calls of brawls, thievery, assaults, and other problems happening in the city because of all the people who had come to town for the census. The chief was about to close the office when his phone rang.

Bureau Chief: *(picking up phone)* Middle Eastern News Services. You heard what? Angels singing? Shepherds on their way into town? New stars in the sky? Listen, buddy, it's been a long, weird day and I'm not in the mood for jokes. What's that? And, this is really on the level? Okay, look, I'll send someone out to check on it, thanks for the tip. *(hangs up phone, calls off left to Reporter)* Hey, Ace, we got a crazy report to check out. Angels singing in the fields, magic stars, and shepherds walking the streets of the city.

Ace: *(Entering from stage left)* Angels in the field, huh? I've heard them. Doo-wop group, performs regularly at the Jerusalem Sands and Casino, right?

Bureau Chief: No. We're talking the wings and halo type of angel. I know. It sounds like a joke, but it's not much crazier than most of the stories we've covered today.

Ace: Okay, being I have no life, I'll check it out. Where do I go?

Bureau Chief: Check the inns. Look for shepherds.

Ace: Shepherds? For this I went to journalism school?

Bureau Chief: You've only got an hour to deadline, so hurry up!

(Bureau Chief exits stage right. Reporter exits off through the audience, then returns to left side of the stage. As he does so, Shepherds enter from left and stand around in a group in front of the stage. Shepherds are talking amongst themselves as the Reporter enters.)

Ace: *(taking out a notebook and pencil)* Okay, I'm with the press, what's going on?

Shepherd 1: The most wonderful thing in the world has happened.

Shepherd 2: A baby has been born!

Shepherd 3: We found him just as the angels told us.

Ace: Wait a second. One at a time. What's all this about a baby?

Shepherd 1: Like the angels said ...

Ace: What angels? Please, just the facts. I've got a deadline.

Shepherd 2: *(trying to calm himself down to tell the story)* We were out in the fields watching the sheep, when all of a sudden the sky became very bright.

(As the Shepherds tell the story, Angels enter from stage left and group themselves on the platform, taking up the whole space. Speaking Angels should be up front. Lights should slowly come down here so, eventually, the only light will be on the platform area. This is to give the illusion of a flashback.)

Shepherd 3: Well, I've got to tell you, we were scared. Then, they started talking to us.

Shepherd 1: Yeah. They said something like "Be not afraid, for behold I bring you ..."

(Angel 1 starts speaking with the Shepherd on "for behold" and then completes the line.)

Angel 1: For behold I bring you good tidings of great joy which shall be to all people ...

Angel 2: For unto you is born this day, in the city of David, a Savior which is Christ the Lord ...

Angel 3: And this shall be a sign unto you, you shall find the babe wrapped in swaddling clothes and laying in a manger.

Angel Choir: Glory to God in the highest. Peace on Earth. Good will toward men.

(Angels exit off right, and the lights slowly come back up.)

Shepherd 4: And then they left. It was my idea to look for the baby.

Shepherd 1: No, it was my idea.

Shepherd 2: Look, it doesn't matter. It was somebody's idea and we came here.

Shepherd 4: And we found the baby *(points to stable)* right there.

Ace: Wait a second. Explain this to me again. All this fuss is for some baby being born in a stable ... in Bethlehem? Do you have any idea how many babies are born each day? Show me a day when a baby isn't born. That would be news.

Shepherd 1: This isn't just any baby. Go inside and look for yourself.

Ace: Okay, I will.

(Shepherds exit left as Reporter walks to right side of stage and steps up to platform. A Maid holding a "door" [cardboard attached to a stick so it can be flipped open and closed] enters from right. Reporter goes up to door and knocks. Maid opens door partway.)

Maid: I'm sorry, sir. We have no rooms.

(Maid starts to shut the door. Reporter stops it with his hand.)

Ace: Why would I want to stay in this crazy house, with shepherds talking nonsense? No, I'm looking for this baby everyone's talking about.

Maid: Baby? I don't know anything about a baby. Let me ask someone. *(calls off left to cook)* Rachel, do you know anything about some baby being here?

(Rachel, a cook at the inn, enters from right, holding a bowl and a spoon. She continues to stir while she talks.)

Rachel: Baby ... hmm ... I haven't seen one. But, I did think it was a little strange when the mistress asked us to send milk down to the barn. And to cook a hot meal for two after the kitchen was closed.

Ace: The barn? You cook for the animals, too?

Rachel: No. I heard we've got people staying there tonight. Let me get the mistress.

(Innkeeper's Wife enters from left. She is instantly suspicious of the Reporter.)

Innkeeper's Wife: Who are you? And why are you asking about the baby?

Ace: I'm a reporter. I've heard a lot of wild stories tonight and I'm just trying to get the lowdown on this so-called miracle baby.

Maid: You're with the press? Oh, dear. With my hair such a mess and in these clothes.

Ace: Don't worry. I didn't bring my camera.

Innkeeper's Wife: I take it you don't believe in miracles. You're just too smart for all that, aren't you?

Ace: It's not a matter of smarts. It's just the way it is. I deal in facts. You want miracles? Call someone from the *Jerusalem Inquirer*. Can I see the baby now?

(Innkeeper's Wife ponders for a moment. It was her that allowed the couple to stay in the stable and she is fiercely protective of them and their baby.)

Innkeeper's Wife: I guess you could go for a few minutes. But they're both very tired. They've walked a long way. And, I won't have you waking that baby. They're back in the stable.

Ace: Do you always put your guests up in such fine housing?

Innkeeper's Wife: *(annoyed)* In case you haven't noticed, the government is running a census. With so many people in town, you can't find a room anywhere. There was nowhere else to put them. The stable is clean and dry, and they have a roof over their heads and soft straw to sleep on. Hey, my husband was going to turn them away. At least this way they had some place to rest.

Ace: All right! All right! Just show me where it is.

Innkeeper's Wife: Not it. Him. Follow me.

(Innkeeper's Wife leads Ace off left. While they are gone, Mary and Joseph enter from right and settle themselves center stage, with a makeshift cradle and a baby. Innkeeper's Wife and Ace, trailed by Rachel and the Maid, reenter through center doors. Innkeeper's Wife points toward Mary and Joseph, then takes a step back as the reporter approaches. A Stable Boy steps forward to block him from entering the barn.)

Stable Boy: What are you doing here? No one comes into this barn.

Innkeeper's Wife: It's okay. I brought him back. Let him see the baby.

(Stable Boy steps back and stands behind the Reporter. All four watch the Reporter approach the baby.)

Ace: *(pulls out notebook and begins to write)* Okay, what's the baby's name?

Joseph: We were told to name him Jesus.

Ace: Told by who?

Mary: An angel.

Ace: More angels. Look, all I see is a baby. A beautiful baby, yes, and like any other parent, I know you think he's extraordinary, but, come on.

Mary: *(laughing)* This isn't us being proud parents. We can't take credit for anything.

Joseph: This child is a fulfillment of a promise made long ago. You're educated ... a lot more educated than I am. So surely you know, God promised us a Savior. Well, as hard as it is for even me to believe, this child is that Savior. Look at my hands. See, these are the hands of a carpenter. A working man. I'm not the type to believe in what I can't touch or see, either. And yet, I swear to you it all happened as the shepherds said.

Mary: Look at him. Can't you see God's love?

(The Reporter looks from the baby to his notebook. Gradually the truth dawns on him. He closes his notebook and runs off the platform.)

Mary: Where are you going?

Ace: To tell the truth to all my readers — I've got a deadline!

(Ace exits off the platform, down center aisle to the back. All others exit right. Narrator comes back to podium.)

Narrator: But when Ace returned to his office and typed up his story, the Bureau Chief refused to run it. He was so sure that Ace had been fooled, that he not only wouldn't use the story, but he fired the reporter. Some time passed and the Bureau Chief forgot about the strange story about a miracle child. Then, he got an anonymous phone tip that a strange star, never before seen had risen in the East. And that three Kings had been seen heading toward Nazareth. Remembering how Ace had fouled up the last time, he decided to follow up this lead himself.

(The Bureau Chief reenters from stage right, Mary and Joseph and the baby reenter from left. Joseph carries in the baby, now in a slightly bigger cradle. Mary holds the "door." Bureau Chief knocks and, in doing so, knocks the door out of Mary's hands.)

Bureau Chief: Okay, I've heard some weird things about a star and some Kings on their way, apparently to see you and the kid. Let me state up front that I won't publish anything about angels or the Son of God. I simply want to know what you know about this star, and who invited these Kings. And, does Herod know they're coming?

Mary: Gee, how about a "Hello, my name is...."?

Bureau Chief: Sorry. I guess that was a bit rude. I'm a reporter and I've come to follow up on a lead. It appears your son has a fan club, including some wealthy scholars from the East. I doubt they're really kings, but you know how the media can distort things.

Joseph: I guess you would know.

Bureau Chief: No, I wouldn't. Because my site only publishes things that we can verify are true.

Mary: Okay — this much is true. A very special star appeared in the sky the night my son was born. It lit the way for those who sought him out then, and I guess it is lighting the way again for these visitors.

Joseph: We don't know who these people are. But I can't say I'm surprised they are coming.

Bureau Chief: You need to explain this to me. In my line of work, one plus one has to equal two.

Mary: You can't apply our logic to God's plans. He can make one plus one equal 75, if he wants to. That's why we need to have faith. It's the only way to bridge the gap and to discover what's really important ... and really true.

Bureau Chief: They won't believe me, you know. The readers, I mean.

Joseph: It's not your job to make them believe. You just have to give them the truth, and God will do the rest.

Bureau Chief: I better go. I have some good news to spread.

(Bureau Chief exits right. Mary picks up baby and she and Joseph exit down the center aisle.)

Advanced Plays

With more sophisticated themes and longer speaking parts, these plays work best for multi-generational productions where youth and adults can take the lead parts

Christmas: Before And After

Characters (in order of appearance)

Narrator	Joseph
Elizabeth	King 1
Mary	King 2
Samuel	King 3

Props

Two chairs
Small table
Medium sized piece of black cloth, plain on one side, stars painted or pinned to other side
Two glasses
"Logs" for fire
Three crowns
Small piece of rope or cord

Notes

"Christmas: Before And After" is simple, spare theater, designed to be performed by a small group of older youth with no set and only a handful of props that are moved around the stage by the cast, and used in different ways in each scene. It is based on improvisations by its original cast and, as such, welcomes adaptation and revision by each group that performs it. Though the narration provides a connecting thread, each individual scene can be performed independent of the others. So, churches could incorporate one scene into worship in the two Sundays leading up to Christmas, and the two Sundays that follow.

(As the play begins, the stage is bare except for one chair upstage center. This is the Narrator's chair, the place he/she will sit when not speaking. Narrator enters and stands center stage. As he/she reads, two of the actors will enter from either side and will set the

table downstage right. Elizabeth will enter from right with a large piece of black material. She sits at the table and spreads the material across it as if it is something she is sewing.)

Narrator: We all think we know the Christmas story. But, the scriptures record only a small sliver of the human history of the Christ Child. What happened with Joseph and Mary before that miraculous night ... and what happened in the many nights that followed it? We may never know for sure, but based on what the Bible tells us, we're going to play a game of "what-if" to try to flesh out four small moments of Jesus' unwritten life story. We hope it might give you a fresher perspective on the Christmas story, and why it's a tale worth telling year after year.

(Mary enters from right and sits at the table.)

Narrator: We start before the birth. The Gospel of Luke tells us that, shortly before the angel visited Mary, her cousin, Elizabeth, found she was going to have a baby. This was something of a miracle in its own right, because Elizabeth was quite elderly, at least by biblical life spans. In this scene, we imagine the meeting between Elizabeth and Mary, after Mary just received the news that she was to bear a son.

Elizabeth: I'm glad you came over. I haven't been getting out much since my third month or so. This body just isn't prepared for these kinds of changes. There's a reason why only young people are supposed to have babies.

Mary: Like me?

Elizabeth: Sure, like you, once you and Joseph get married ... wait a second, you don't mean *now*, do you? Oh, wait until I get a hold of that Joseph. I'd send your uncle after him but, since he heard the news about me, he can't even speak, poor guy!

Mary: No ... Joseph didn't do anything.

120

Elizabeth: You don't mean you've....

Mary: No, I haven't "known" anyone, Elizabeth. I know this is hard to believe, but I was visited by an angel who told me that I've been chosen to have a very special child. He's going to be the Son of God.

Elizabeth: Mary, I know your mother. She's not going to believe that story anymore than I do. And what did Joseph say?

Mary: Well, he was a little freaked out. You know, he's older and he's got a reputation to think about. But, I think he believes me.

Elizabeth: I think you should tell me about this "angel." *(makes quotation mark gestures)*

Mary: Well, it was the most amazing thing. I was sweeping up the house, when this person, all in white, just sort of appeared. I chased him around with the broom for a while. I thought he was some intruder, sneaking in to steal food. But, he kept talking quietly to me, and I soon realized that he was an angel. Then he said I was going to have a baby, so I chased him around some more, because I'm not that kind of girl. He finally made me understand. This child has a very special purpose, and I guess he needs a special introduction to this world.

Elizabeth: Five months ago I would have said you were crazy, but then five months ago I never thought I'd be a mother. I believe you.

Mary: Thank you so much! Could I stay with you for a little while ... 'til I know Joseph is really sure about this? I don't know if he believes me.

Elizabeth: Of course you can stay.

Mary: The funny thing is, I can't get over this feeling that I won't be having the baby here in Nazareth.

121

Elizabeth: Don't be silly, child. Where else would you have it? In Bethlehem? Joseph's family hasn't lived there in years.

(Narrator steps forward and snaps fingers. As he does, Elizabeth picks up cloth and hands it to one of the "King actors," then exits stage right. Mary moves table to stage left, then exits stage left. Another "King actor" moves the chairs downstage center and turns them around, so the backs are to the audience. The other "King actor" drapes the cloth, black side facing out, then both exit.)

Narrator: Meanwhile, on the other side of town, Joseph was trying to sort everything out with his friend, Samuel.

(Joseph enters from stage right, Samuel from stage left. Each is holding a glass. They sit on the edge of the platform center stage, just in front of the draped chairs.)

Samuel: What's the matter, Joe? You look a little out of it.

Joseph: I've had kind of a bad week. *(hesitates a moment)* Mary is ... expecting.

Samuel: Expecting what? I thought everything was settled with you two.

Joseph: I mean she told me she's having a baby.

Samuel: Congratulations ... *(notices Joseph does not look happy)* ... or not....

Joseph: She told me that the child is the Son of God ... no jokes, please. I'm very serious. I came to you because you always give good advice. I was thinking maybe I shouldn't marry her. Maybe I should find some safe place to send her, where no one would make trouble for her.

Samuel: Well, that would probably be the smart thing. Son of God, I mean, that doesn't happen every day.... But, what if she's telling the truth and you leave her and ... well, it messes everything up ... for you, for her, for the whole world? Wow, dude, I wouldn't want to be in your shoes then.

Joseph: *(glaring)* You're not helping. It gets more complicated. The other night, this white-robed person suddenly appeared in my room and told me not to worry. He said that Mary was telling the truth. That I should marry her, and that this child *was* going to be the Savior of the world.

Samuel: I knew it. I knew you were messing with the world if you did the wrong thing. I haven't had too many of them, but that sounds like a sign.

Joseph: *(sarcastically)* Ya think? Look, I want to believe it, but the thing is, what are people going to say?

Samuel: You have the opportunity to parent a miracle child and you care about the small town gossip of a few peasants?

Joseph: You're right, of course. I do love Mary. And, I trust her. But, how do you bring up the Son of God? I mean, what kind of father do I have to be? What do I do?

Samuel: Love him, protect him, teach him ... and let God do the rest.

(The two clink glasses, as the Narrator moves forward and gestures for Joseph and Samuel to exit. Joseph exits left, Samuel right. Narrator takes cloth off chair and waves it in a circle, representing the passage of time, as the Kings enter, crowns in place. One carries "logs" for their fire. They sit on the floor in front of the stage.)

Narrator: Now we fast forward to the "after" portion of our story. Jesus has been born. The angels have sung their song. The shepherds visited the manger, and the Wise Men have made their visit.

Trouble is brewing in Jerusalem as a sick and jealous Herod begins to foresee a possible rival. We catch up with the Wise Men after they've left the child. They've camped for the night and are sharing a meal. *(re-drapes cloth over the shares, this time with the "star side" facing out)*

King 1: Tomorrow, we set out for home. I was thinking, maybe we should try a different route.

King 2: A different route? It's going to be hard enough to make this journey now that the star has left us. Our maps don't list half these towns.

King 1: Still, I think we have to go another way. You see, I know this sounds weird, but, I had a dream last night.

King 3: In your dream, did you see a tall man, all in white, who spoke to you in a deep voice?

King 1: Yes! How did you know?

King 3: I had the same dream.

King 2: Uh ... so did I. He warned me that all of us, and the child, would die if we went back to Herod.

King 3: Did you see how Herod was going to slaughter all the babies around Bethlehem to try to find the child? And we couldn't warn Mary and Joseph?

King 1: *(shuddering)* Yes.

King 2: Ditto. Okay ... I guess it's agreed. We need to find another route home. But, I don't think we have nearly enough supplies. And, none of us know this country very well. Without the star, how will we know which way to go?

King 1: Before we leave tomorrow, we'll send our servants into town. Herod won't know them and they should be able to purchase all we need. I brought our star charts with us. That will keep us headed east.

King 3: Look, a star is beginning to rise in the eastern sky. Perhaps that is how God will see us safely home.

(Kings pick up the campfire and exit right, as Elizabeth enters from right, and Joseph and Mary from left. Joseph, who has a small piece of rope with him, lifts up the fabric, reverses it so the stars are on the inside, then loops the rope around the top to make it look like a bag. Mary and Elizabeth each grab one chair, and place them by the table, stage left.)

Narrator: There was one more dream to come. A warning to Joseph that he must get the young child out of Herod's reach.

Joseph: We need to talk. We have to pack up and leave now.

Mary: What do you mean? We just set up our home. I made curtains. And, Jesus is too little to travel.

Joseph: Jesus will be dead if we don't go.

Mary: What? What's going to happen to my baby?

Joseph: I had a dream last night. An angel visited me and he warned me that Herod was going to kill the child if we stay here. I just sold my store and any tool I can't carry. It should be enough to get us away from here.

Mary: But, my family is here. Everyone I know is here.

Joseph: I know this isn't easy. But, the angels have been right all along. I don't think this is the time to question them. Herod's crazy, Mary. Remember when he made us go back to Bethlehem for that census? I don't even like Bethlehem. This guy will do anything. If he gets it in his head that our baby is going to do anything to threaten his throne, he's going to kill him. I won't rest until Jesus is out of his clutches.

Mary: But where can we go?

Joseph: Egypt. Herod has no authority there. He can't hurt the baby if we make it there.

Mary: Egypt? They don't worship like us. They have all those strange gods and they don't particularly like Jews.

Joseph: The angel told me we would be safe there. But, we'll be cautious. We'll keep to ourselves and we'll worship in secret. And, I can find carpentry work anywhere, so I know I can support us there.

Mary: Okay, Joseph. You're right. We need to keep believing in what the angels tell us.

Joseph: We'll be fine. I'm sure of it.

(Mary and Joseph exit off left with the black cloth. Other actors enter and remove chairs and table as Narrator speaks.)

Narrator: The Bible tells us that Mary and Joseph made the trip to Egypt safely, and remained there until word reached them that Herod had died. It was just one time of many when Joseph followed the advice of our fictional friend, Samuel, to "Love him, protect him, teach him ... and let God do the rest." If our four little scenarios have one thing in common is that all the people in these stories made pretty dramatic leaps of faith, and acted on the Word of God even when it flew in the face of customs, other people's judgments, even risking own their lives. We hope that this is the message you take away from here today. Let's all listen for that little voice inside. It could be that God may be telling you something. And when he does, perhaps the courage and faith of Mary, Joseph, and the Wise Men will encourage you to find a new way home.

"Unto Us A Child Is Born ... Next, On Omar"

Characters (in order of appearance)

Jacob	Wise Man 1
Omar Looseandfree	Wise Man 2
Applause Child (nonspeaking)	Wise Man 3
Shepherd 1	Servant (nonspeaking)
Shepherd 2	Mary
Shepherd 3	Joseph
Lead Angel	Audience Member 2
2nd Angel	Audience Member 3
Angel Choir	Stage Manager
Audience Member 1	Stagehands (nonspeaking)

Props

Four chairs
Handheld microphones (real or fake)
Sign with "Applause" written on it
Bells
Three pillows
Baby doll

Notes

Another one of our "intentional anachronism plays," "Unto Us A Child Is Born ... Next, On Omar" imagines how a very contemporary talk show might have covered the events surrounding the birth of Christ. In keeping with the "sound stage" look, the set is very basic, consisting of three chairs placed downstage center. Another chair, for the Applause Child, is placed just off stage right. One or two handheld microphones are needed, one for Omar, and one for Jacob, who will take the audience questions. Three cast members should be planted in the audience.

Because of its somewhat sophisticated take on the story, this play is best suited for a youth group presentation, though older elementary children can cover some of the parts. Please note that if females are cast as the talk show host and announcer, the names of Omar and Jacob can be changed. In its original production, both parts were played by women.

———————

(Stage is empty at opening. Jacob enters from stage right, with a hand mike.)

Jacob: And now, from downtown Bethlehem, home of the House of David, it's the known world's favorite talk show, "Omar!" And now, here's your host, Omar Looseandfree.

(Small child walks in from stage right with an "Applause" sign as Omar enters from stage left with hand mike. If the audience doesn't applaud, the child should point to the sign and say, "Can't you read?" Child then sits on chair, next to the platform, stage right.)

Omar: Thank you, thank you. It's good to see all of you after our two-week vacation. Yeah, we were off in Jerusalem for a bit, doing that census thing to register, just like everybody else. That's right, even celebrities had to do it. You'd think being on television would give you *some* privileges. But, Jacob tells me you had a bit of mob scene here, right Jacob?

Jacob: That's right. I was lucky. I was born right here, so I could stay in my own house. Even made a few bucks renting the stable out back. There weren't even rooms at the inns for all the people, and some of them just wandered the streets all night. And a few of them had some pretty wild stories to tell.

Omar: Wild stories. Well, here's our answer for Sweeps Week. Anyway, that leads us to our topic for tonight, "People Who Came To Bethlehem Because Of A Vision." First up, let's welcome a group of shepherds.

(Applause Child holds up sign. Shepherds enter from stage left and sit on the three chairs. They appear nervous and a bit confused.)

Omar: *(speaking slowly and calmly)* Thank you for coming to talk to us, Shepherds. Now, just relax, and tell us, what happened to bring you here tonight?

Shepherd 1: Well, it all started a few nights ago. We were out in the field, watching the sheep. And, you know, that's pretty hard work. *(gaining courage)* A lot harder than talking into a microphone every night.

Shepherd 2: Those sheep wander all over. They're always getting lost. Getting their paws caught in brambles. And, they never sleep when they should.

Shepherd 3: We finally got them all together and we were trying to eat our dinner when we heard a sound.

Omar: What kind of sound?

Shepherd 1: I've tended sheep a long time, and I've never heard a sound like this. It sounded like ... tinkling bells ... and singing.

(Angels enter from stage right, ringing bells and singing "Glory." Several cluster on the steps next to the stage. Others come up and stand behind where the Shepherds are seated. Shepherds react to the "memory" with fear and trembling.)

Shepherd 2: Who are you? And what do you want?

Shepherd 3: *(jumps off chair and curls up in a ball)* Make them go away!

Lead Angel: Do not be afraid! For behold, I bring you good tidings of great joy!

2nd Angel: *(leaning over the hiding Shepherds)* Which shall be to all people — even you!

129

(Shepherds sit up and watch.)

Lead Angel: For unto you is born this day, in the city of David, a Savior which is Christ the Lord.

2nd Angel: *(standing up and stepping forward)* And this shall be a sign unto you. You shall find the baby wrapped in swaddling clothes, and lying in a manger.

Shepherd 2: And then, we turned around and saw that those Angels were not alone. They had brought friends. There were angels everywhere you looked. And they were singing ... on key!

(Angels move off steps and spread themselves across the front of the platform.)

Angel Choir: Glory to God in the highest. Peace on Earth, good will to men.

(Angels then move quickly off stage right.)

Shepherd 3: And, just like that *(snaps fingers)* they were gone!

Omar: *(genuinely amazed, also snaps fingers)* Just like that?

Shepherd 3: *(snaps fingers)* Just like that!

Omar: Wow! *(to audience)* What do you think, guys? Some vision, huh? Well, what did you do then?

Shepherd 1: Well, we knew the city of David was Bethlehem. Shepherds aren't all that dumb, you know. And we knew Bethlehem was about a day's journey from where we were.

Shepherd 2: So we gathered up the sheep and we headed toward Bethlehem. Funny thing. It was like those sheep knew something special was happening, because they didn't give us a hard time rounding them up.

Shepherd 3: And just like the Angels said, we found the baby lying in a manger, with animals all around him, and he was all wrapped up like a mummy.

Shepherd 2: That was the swaddling clothes, dummy! And, besides, his head wasn't covered.

Omar: Okay, okay, let's cool it. Our "Shepherds Who Just Can't Get Along" show is next week. Let's take some questions from the audience.

(Audience Member 1 stands up, from front row of audience. Jacob walks over with microphone.)

Audience Member 1: Yes. First, I just want to tell that second shepherd that I think he shouldn't be making fun of his coworker. That can really wreck company morale. So, try to be a little more tolerant, okay? Anyway, my question is, you went all that distance just because some angels told you to?

Shepherd 3: You want to argue with angels?

Audience Member 1: *(taken aback)* I guess not. Well, thank you. *(sits down)*

Omar: Okay. Thank you, Shepherds. Everyone, let's give a hand for the Shepherds.

(Shepherds exit stage left.)

Omar: Now, we have three kings who've taken an even bigger leap of faith. Let's welcome them.

(Applause Child steps forward with sign. Wise Men enter up center aisle slowly, regally. They are accompanied by a Servant, who runs ahead and places pillows on the three chairs, bows deeply, notices Omar and Jacob have not bowed, and clears throat loudly, indicating that they should. Omar and Jacob hastily also bow until Wise Men are all seated.)

131

Omar: Well, your highnesses, so kind of you to join us. You're not from around here, are you?

Wise Man 1: Well, let me make one correction. We're not really Kings. We're just very learned men who have earned the respect and adoration of others because of our knowledge, and our ability to see and understand things others don't. We watch the stars to tell us things about our world.

Wise Man 2: When the winds will change.

Wise Man 3: I'm working on using the stars to foretell the weather.

Omar: Now that would be great. We could use that. I know our weather soothsayers haven't been doing too well lately. So, what should we call you?

Wise Man 3: Wise men would be fine.

Omar: *(calling off to Jacob)* Remind me to fire my crack research team tomorrow. *(to Wise Men)* But, please, tell your story.

Wise Man 1: When I viewed the stars that night, I found one I could not identify on my charts.

Wise Man 2: None of us could.

Wise Man 1: I watched the star for several nights and realized it was moving.

Wise Man 2: We couldn't explain it.

Wise Man 3: I remembered reading in the ancient prophecies that a star would appear in the East. And that it would lead us to a new king.

Omar: A new king, huh? What did Herod think about that?

Wise Man 1: Well, we stopped by to see him, of course. We wanted to know if he knew where this king was, but he hadn't heard anything. He seemed as curious as all of us were.

Wise Man 2: More than curious, as we later found out.

Wise Man 1: He practically ordered us to find this king, so he could go worship him, too.

Wise Man 2: We continued to follow the star, so we could deliver our gifts.

Omar: So, what sort of gifts do you give a king?

Wise Man 2: We brought him gold, frankincense, and myrrh.

Wise Man 3: I suggested the myrrh. I like the smell.

Jacob: It is different ... more along the lines of "Caravan" than "Camel No. 5."

Omar: *(giving a dirty look to Jacob for butting in)* Excuse me. The last time I looked, this show wasn't called "Jacob"! *(turning back to Wise Men)* But, myrrh is usually used to prepare bodies for burial, isn't it? Kind of a morbid gift for a baby.

Wise Man 1: Are you questioning the wisdom of a Wise Man?

Omar: *(genuinely humbled)* No, of course not. Never.

Wise Man 2: There's more to the gift of myrrh than just a nice smell. It symbolizes the supreme sacrifice this boy will be called to make for us when he becomes a man.

Omar: That sounds like another show. So, where did the star finally take you?

Wise Man 1: We found him in a stable. Such a terrible place for a king.

Wise Man 2: All those animals ... and he was sleeping on hay. Not a fitting place.

Wise Man 3: Oh, I don't know. I thought it was kind of warm and cozy. And the innkeeper and his wife made sure it was very clean. The hay was freshly pitched, not the same stuff the animals had been chewing. It was serene and quiet and, now I know this sounds crazy, but I even felt like the animals were in awe of it all. They just kept watching the baby and making quiet, contented little noises.

Jacob: The animals even noticed? Hey, Omar, how about that topic for tomorrow's show? "Animals That Kept Watch Over A King."

Omar: *(with a withering look)* How about "Talk Show Announcers Living In Barns Because They Kept Upstaging The Star"?

Jacob: I think I'll go check on our next guests. *(exits stage right)*

Omar: *(to the Wise Men)* Sorry about that. Please, continue.

Wise Man 3: The prophecies say this king will be "a man of sorrows, and acquainted with grief." I think the humble setting couldn't have been more perfect.

Wise Man 1: There is a lot of truth in that, I guess. Anyway, we gave the child our gifts.

Wise Man 3: And we told the parents what Herod had said. But then, as we were starting back, I had a very troubling dream. An Angel warned me not to return to Herod because, out of his jealousy, he would harm the new king and us.

Wise Man 1: We tend to believe his dreams. They usually are right.

Wise Man 2: Unlike his weather forecasts.

Wise Man 1: So, we've mapped out a different route and we'll be going home another way.

Wise Man 2: Speaking of which, we should be going.

Wise Man 3: Yes, we have a long journey ahead ... and, besides, our camels are double-parked.

Omar: Well, thank you for being on our show. Ladies and gentlemen, a big hand for the Wise Men.

(Wise Men once again exit up the center aisle.)

Omar: I don't know. Shepherds seeing visions. Kings dreaming dreams. Either everyone has gone crazy, or something really miraculous has happened in this little town. Maybe our final guests can clear up the mystery. Our staff caught them just as they appeared to be packing for a trip, and they agreed to appear on this program. Here they are, the family that caused all the fuss, Mary, Joseph, and the baby.

(Applause Child again holds up sign. Mary, Joseph, and the baby enter from stage right, and sit. Mary holds the baby tight and gazes somewhat nervously at the audience.)

Omar: Mary, Joseph. I can't thank you enough for coming to visit with us.

Joseph: We can't stay long. We have to get to Egypt very soon.

Mary: The dream the Wise Men talked about? Joseph had the same dream. God told us to take our baby and move to Egypt because Herod means to harm him.

Joseph: We don't know exactly what Herod is cooking up, but he's probably so jealous of some other king coming to take his place, he could try to kill our son — and maybe kill a lot of other little boys trying to find him. I don't want to take any chances. He's too special already. *(smiles and kisses the baby on the head)*

(Omar, Jacob, and Applause Child crowd around the child. The Shepherds appear on the steps, and Omar waves to them to come up.)

Omar: He is very sweet.

Mary: And too important for all of us to allow any harm to come to him. This baby has a special destiny. He's mine, but he really belongs to all human beings everywhere. I mean, an Angel told me he was coming.

Omar: What did you name him, Mary?

Mary: We call him Jesus.

Omar: Not a common name. What made you choose it?

Mary: The Angel told me that was to be his name. It's a name that carries some pretty heavy baggage. The Angel also told me that it meant he would save the people from their sins. *(nodding to Shepherds)* We don't argue with Angels, either.

Omar: I know you two are in a hurry, but our audience must have a bunch of questions about all this. Can you just answer a few?

(Mary looks toward Joseph who appears anxious, but finally nods his head "okay." Jacob heads out to the audience with microphone.)

Audience Member 2: Wasn't this king foretold in the prophecies supposed to be a descendent of David?

Mary: Joseph is from David's family.

Audience Member 3: Joseph, what do you do for a living?

Joseph: I'm a carpenter.

Audience Member 3: No offense, but if this is the Messiah we've all been waiting for, don't you think God would have chosen a more distinguished family member as a father? You know, one of the chief priests, or a leader of the temple, or at least a wealthy merchant?

Joseph: No offense taken. I know I'm one of the humblest branches of the "Jesse Tree." But, I think you're missing the point here, just like Herod. Jesus didn't come to be a human king ... someone who'll knock Herod off the throne and rule in a great palace.

Mary: Jesus' kingdom is not of this world, but of heaven. He didn't come just for the wealthy merchants, but for the shepherds, and the innkeepers, and the farmers, and the people that run the poorest stall in the marketplace ... even for the beggars, and drunks, and thieves ... *(looking at Omar)* and shallow, sleazy, but not soulless talk show hosts.

Jacob: Amen.

Omar: Mary, Joseph, I know you have to leave now. My staff has arranged for you to have a safe escort out of the city and on into Egypt. And, thank you for sharing this very special child with all of us.

(Mary, Joseph, Baby, Shepherds, and Applause Child all exit stage right.)

Omar: *(struggling to find the words)* What do you know friends? For once in my life, I'm speechless. I put this show together because I thought it would be good for a few laughs. I mean, come on

137

... all these visions, and angels and stuff. We're all so sophisticated now; we think we're beyond the power of miracles. But I truly believe, after what I've seen and heard tonight, that these events are miracles, and that God has given us a very special gift. Remember, giving the gift is only part of the action. It isn't truly a gift until it is opened, accepted, and acknowledged with thanks. We must welcome the gift of this child by opening our hearts to him, accepting him as our Savior, and thanking God by living the way he wants us to live. Good night, everyone.

(Stage Manager's voice is heard offstage, saying "And, we're off the air." Stagehands enter and remove the chairs.)

Jacob: *(walking over to Omar and giving him a hug)* Good show, Omar. I think this may be our best one yet.

Omar: I think so, too. You know, it was so good, maybe we should make the gift of this child an annual celebration.

Jacob: Yeah! Like a holiday. We could call it "Jesus Is Born Day."

Omar: We're going to need a catchier name than that. All right, we'll work on it.

(Arm in arm. Omar and Jacob exit stage right.)

The Word Made Flesh

Characters (in order of appearance)

Father (Aaron)	Innkeeper (Daniel)
Benjamin	Innkeeper's Wife
Esther	Leah
Mother	Innkeeper's Child 1
Rebecca	Innkeeper's Child 2
Ruth	First Shepherd
Joseph	Second Shepherd
Mary	Third Shepherd

Props
Two tables
Four chairs
Door
Scrolls
Broom
Pitcher of water
Glasses
Tray with food and bowls on it
Blanket
Towel
Manger
Star

Notes

This play draws together ancient prophecies from the book of Isaiah and the birth of Jesus, showing how his coming was a fulfillment of those prophecies. It has sixteen speaking parts, four of which are best for little ones, another four which should be played by teens or adults, and the remaining suitable for children in-between. The lead role of Esther was written for a girl about twelve.

The stage setup includes a table, downstage left, with chairs on either side. A second table is set upstage on the right with several chairs. A door needs to be placed at one side for entering and exiting.

(The play opens in the kitchen of a house just outside of Bethlehem. At the table stage right, a young boy sits with his Father. On the table are a number of scrolls. Father is attempting to teach his son the ancient prophecies, but the boy, Benjamin, would rather be out in the field, tending the cattle and playing with his friends. A young girl, Esther, is in front of the stage, sweeping.)

Father: So, as the prophet Isaiah says, "The people that walked in darkness have seen a great light; they that dwell in the land of the shadow of death, upon them hath the light shined."

Benjamin: Yeah, yeah, yeah. And speaking of light, there isn't going to be much left out there and I think I should go get the cattle in ...

Father: We have at least one more hour. Now tell me ... what does this mean to us?

Benjamin: *(thinking very hard)* That God is going to make the sun shine longer? That would be great. Think how much more time we can spend outdoors.

Father: No. Benjamin, you need to concentrate.

Esther: *(who has been listening)* That God will not make us suffer long. That he will send the light to deliver us from the darkness of oppression. From people like the Romans who persecute us.

Father: *(to the daughter)* Excellent. Esther, you would make an excellent scholar. I wish your brother had such a mind.

Benjamin: *(getting up)* Great. So teach her and let me go out to the fields.

Father: You know it's not our way to teach girls. Though sometimes I wonder why. Esther can recite these prophecies in her sleep, while you're more concerned about our cows. Don't you know that these teachings are the only things that have sustained us through centuries of oppression and injustice?

Benjamin: I'm sorry, Father. I just don't see how learning what a bunch of dead guys said is going to make the Romans go away and make our life any easier.

Father: All right. Go tend to your cows. We'll come back to this tomorrow. But, you must promise me you'll work harder at this.

Benjamin: I promise. *(runs off right)*

Father: Esther, come sit with me. It's not our way to teach girls, but your mind is too good to waste. Come, talk with me.

Esther: Father, do you think we'll live to see that great light?

Father: God doesn't tell us when the prophecy will be fulfilled. If not in our time, perhaps in your children's time.

Esther: So, we're looking for a child. And we know it will be of the lineage of David.

Father: You have been paying attention. As Isaiah says, "And there shall come forth a rod out of the stem of Jesse, and a branch shall grow out of his roots."

Esther: Well, that means, he could be born right here. Isn't this the ancient home of David's family?

Father: I've often thought that. Every time a child is born I go to visit it and wonder, is this the one?

141

(Mother enters stage left, along with two younger children, Rebecca and Ruth.)

Mother: Esther, I know how much you like talking prophecy with your father. But, we have a house full of people coming tonight and I need your help with dinner.

Rebecca: Uncle Eli and his family are coming from Jerusalem.

Ruth: And, Aunt Rachael's family from Nazareth.

Mother: I don't know where we're going to put everyone. Why do those Romans need to count us all anyway?

Father: So they can raise our taxes, of course. *(to Esther)* Go help your mother.

Rebecca: *(to her mother)* What's taxes?

Mother: Money we have to pay to the government.

Ruth: What's a government?

Mother: You children ask too many questions. You all take after your father with all his books. Come, we have vegetables to slice and a chicken to cook.

Rebecca: I'm not cutting the onions. They make me cry.

(Mother and the young children exit left. Esther starts to leave, then takes a step back.)

Esther: One thing, though. This baby will be different, right?

Father: Well, Isaiah does say, "The Lord himself shall give you a sign. Behold a virgin shall conceive and bear a son." That would certainly be a bit unusual.

Esther: Just so I know what to look for.

(Esther and Mother exit stage left. Father returns to his scrolls. Mary and Joseph come up the center aisle. They have already been to several inns and have found no room. They are both exhausted. They come up toward the front and pretend to knock. Father gets up to answer the door.)

Father: Can I help you?

Joseph: Yes, sir. I was wondering if you might know of another inn. We've tried just about every one in town.

Father: Well, you know about the census. I'm afraid all the rooms are rented.

Joseph: That's why we're here. My family is from here. But we've lived in Nazareth for many years, and no one still lives here that we can stay with. My wife is about to have a child.

Father: I can see that. Here, come in and sit down. *(Mary and Joseph sit on the edge of the stage; Father calls offstage)* Esther, please bring some water. I'm sorry I can't offer you a place to stay. My wife and I have family coming in tonight. We simply have no room. But I have a friend, Daniel, who runs a small inn just up the road. Perhaps he can find a place for you. Tell him that Aaron sent you.

Mary: Thank you, sir. You've been very kind.

(Esther enters with a pitcher of water. Both Mary and Joseph drink.)

Esther: You're here for the census?

Mary: Yes, my husband, Joseph, is part of the lineage of David. He's very proud of that. But today, I wish he'd been born to a family that lived a bit closer to Nazareth.

Joseph: Are you ready to travel again?

Mary: Yes. *(hands the pitcher back to Esther)* Thank you.

(Mary and Joseph exit back up the center aisle, then come back down the left aisle.)

Esther: Did you hear that, Father? He is from David's family. And, she's going to have a baby.

Father: Relax, child. Don't be looking for Messiahs everywhere.

Esther: But you said you do.

Father: I know. But if this was the child, don't you think God would at least provide a place for him to be born?

Esther: As you always tell me, God doesn't always do things the way we think he will. I was thinking. Even if they find a room at the inn, they may be short on blankets. Could I bring them one after supper?

Father: We barely have enough blankets to cover everyone who'll be staying here.

Esther: She can have mine.

Father: You're a good child. After supper, and only if your mother says it's all right.

Esther: Thanks, Father.

(Esther and Father exit left. Innkeeper, his Wife and Daughters enter and sit at the table stage right. Mary and Joseph reenter from the aisle and knock at the door.)

Innkeeper: Now what. Can't I even eat my dinner?

Innkeeper's Wife: We're out of rooms and my kitchen is closed. Send them away.

Innkeeper's Child 1: I'll get it.

Innkeeper's Wife: Oh, no, you won't. Not with all the crazy people coming into town this week. You let your father get it.

(Innkeeper gets up and opens the door.)

Innkeeper: I'm sorry. We're all full.

Mary: Please, sir. We've tried every other place and I just can't go another step. Your friend, Aaron, said you might find something for us.

Innkeeper: You know Aaron?

Joseph: We just met him. He was kind enough to give us a drink.

(Leah gets up and stands behind him. The little ones follow just behind her.)

Innkeeper: He is a very good man. But we have no rooms.

Leah: Father, what about the stable? It's clean and dry.

Innkeeper's Child 2: Just a little smelly.

Innkeeper: Shhh. No place in my inn is smelly. The stable is very clean. Would that be all right?

Joseph: That would be fine.

Innkeeper: *(to Leah)* Take them back and make them comfortable. And, ask your mother if there isn't something we can give them to eat.

Innkeeper's Wife: I heard you. Daniel, I sometimes think you're too good a man. There's some bread, and I think I have some cheese. I'll prepare something.

Innkeeper Child 1: They didn't look like crazy people.

Innkeeper's Wife: Do you have to repeat everything I say? Hush now, help me clear the table.

(Innkeeper's Wife stands, pushes the table back and exits stage right with the children. Innkeeper follows. Leah leads Mary and Joseph onto the stage and settles them on the floor, center stage.)

Leah: My mother will have something for you to eat soon. Is there anything I can get you?

Mary: It's a bit chilly, would you have a blanket?

Leah: I'm sorry. All our blankets are being used. Perhaps I can get you one of my father's cloaks?

Mary: It's all right. We'll make do.

(Innkeeper's Wife enters with a tray.)

Innkeeper's Wife: I found some fruit, as well as the bread and cheese, and I've warmed up a little soup. If you need anything else, just tell Leah. *(points to daughter)*

(Leah and her mother exit stage right. At stage left, Esther enters holding a blanket.)

Esther: *(calling offstage)* Mother, I've finished the dishes. Is there anything else you need?

Mother: *(entering from stage left, wiping her hands on a towel)* No. Thank you. You were a big help. And thanks for getting your

146

sisters to bed. They were so excited I thought they'd never fall asleep. Why are you holding a blanket?

Esther: Well, this woman. She stopped by with her husband before. She's having a baby and they had no place to stay. Father sent them to Daniel's inn and they're so full that I thought she might need a blanket.

Mother: And what are you going to sleep under?

Esther: My cloak?

Mother: Do what you want, but don't complain to me if you get cold.

(Mother exits stage left. Esther runs down center aisle, around the back and up the right aisle. She knocks on the door of the inn. Leah answers.)

Leah: Esther? What are you doing here? Don't you realize how late it is?

Esther: I'm sorry, Leah. But, the woman who's going to have the baby ... is she here?

Leah: Yes, she's out in the stable. Oh, that's right. She stopped by your house.

Esther: I brought a blanket. I thought, with your house so full, that you wouldn't have an extra.

Leah: We didn't. I'm glad you brought this. I'll take you to them. *(looking past Esther)* Who is that?

(Shepherds begin walking up the center aisle.)

Esther: They look like shepherds.

147

Leah: *(yelling out to the Shepherds)* Who are you? Why are you here? My father doesn't rent rooms to shepherds.

First Shepherd: We're not here for a room. We're here to see the child.

Esther: The child? Did she have the baby?

Leah: I don't know. She hadn't when I saw her last.

Second Shepherd: Some angels visited us out in the fields. They told us to go seek the child born tonight. We followed that star *(pointing up)* and it stopped right over this place.

Leah: *(to Esther)* You see, this is why my father won't rent rooms to shepherds. All that time alone in the field, they get a little odd.

Third Shepherd: I know what you think. But, we're not crazy, and we haven't been drinking. Angels did visit us. It was the brightest light I had ever seen. And we were scared. But they told us, "Fear not. For behold, I bring you good tidings of great joy, which shall be to all people."

Second Shepherd: "For unto you is born this day in the city of David, a Savior which is Christ the Lord. And this shall be a sign unto you, you shall find the baby wrapped in swaddling clothes and lying in a manger."

Esther: *(to herself)* "The people that walked in darkness have seen a great light ... For unto you a child is born, unto us a son is given." *(to Leah)* Leah, take us to the stable now.

(Leah walks down the steps and leads Esther and the Shepherds to center stage, where "Baby Jesus" now is. The shepherds immediately kneel. Esther comes up to Mary and hands her the blanket.)

Esther: I thought you might need this.

Mary: How thoughtful. Come see the baby.

(Esther looks down at the child.)

Esther: Can I ask you something that's kind of personal? You don't have to answer if you don't want.

Mary: Ask me.

Esther: Was this a special child? I mean ... was there anything different about his birth?

Mary: Well, let's see. An angel told me he would be born. Scared me to death at first. Then, Joseph wasn't sure he should marry me because ...

Esther: "Behold, a virgin shall conceive...."

Joseph: *(clearly impressed)* You know your prophecy.

Leah: What are you talking about?

Esther: Don't you understand? This is the one. This is the child that the prophets foretold. I have to tell my father.

(Esther exits stage left.)

Shepherd 1: I hope you don't mind that we came. But the angels told us to seek the child.

Joseph: We don't mind. We're glad you came. But, now that you've seen the child, I think you should go and tell others what you've seen.

Shepherd 2: He's right. This is something we need to share.

(Shepherds stand and turn to leave.)

Shepherd 3: We'll come back later, and we'll bring you some food.

(Shepherds start to exit up center aisle.)

Shepherd 1: We'd better go check on the sheep first.

Shepherd 2: You can go back and check on the sheep. We'll go in to town.

Shepherd 1: Why don't I ever get to go into town?

Shepherd 3: Honestly? Because people think you're a little weird ... you talk to the sheep too much.

Leah: Esther knows a lot more about that prophecy stuff than I do. Can you tell me why she's so excited?

Joseph: Because, a long time ago, God made a promise to us. To send someone who would lead us out of darkness to the light of salvation. This child is God's way of keeping that promise.

Leah: Wow, all that for just one baby? I mean, he can't even feed himself, how is he going to lead anyone?

Mary: *(laughing)* Well, obviously, it's going to take a little time.

(Esther reenters out of breath, tugging at her Father's sleeve.)

Esther: *(pointing to the child)* See, Father, there he is ... the child, born unto us ... he's everything the prophets said ...

Father: Yes, I see that. *(to Mary and Joseph)* You don't know what this means to me. How long I've waited to see this moment. I didn't think it would happen in my lifetime.

Joseph: It's not going to be an easy road ahead for him, or for any of us. But, at last, God's work on earth has begun. *(to Esther)* Why don't you put your blanket over the baby? It's getting a bit chilly.

Father: It's also quite late. Your wife and the child need to rest. It's been quite a busy day.

Leah: I should get inside anyway. Mom is probably worried. Gee, wait till I tell her we've got a Savior in our stable. No other inn can claim that.

(Leah exits stage right. Father and Esther begin walking up the center aisle.)

Esther: Father, what did the man mean when he said, "It's not going to be an easy road ahead" for the baby? If he came to be a king, if he's the chosen one, won't God make everything easy for him?

Father: Child, you have a lot more prophecy to learn.

Miracles? No Problem!

Characters (in order of appearance)

Elizabeth	Mary 2
Mary	Shepherd 1
Gabriel	Shepherd 2
King 1	Shepherd 3
King 2	2nd Angel
King 3	3rd Angel
Mary's Mother	Angel Choir
Joseph	

Props

Stool/chair
Bowl
Star
Broom
Sack
Carrots and veggies
Knife
Handkerchief
Bundle

Notes

This play puts the viewer in Mary's home the day she received the news that she was to have a special child, and is based on Luke 1:26-38. It envisions Gabriel arriving in Mary's kitchen and Mary's reaction to the news. As he talks with Mary and tells her what will be, various scenes from the Christmas story are acted out on the other side of the stage, giving Mary a glimpse of her future.

The play has fourteen speaking parts, with parts for all, from seven or eight years old through adults, plus the Angel Choir, which offers a chance to dress up all the little ones in the Sunday school and bring them onstage to say one line in unison.

(Stage is empty at the beginning of the play, except for one stool or plain chair that is slightly right of center, a bowl that sits on the platform, a broom that rests against the platform, stage right, and a hanging star. All the "vision" scenes will occur stage left. The play was initially performed in a sanctuary with a raised platform. Mary was on the floor level, and Gabriel above her on the platform. From stage right, Elizabeth enters, carrying a sack.)

Elizabeth: *(calling off)* Mary? Are you home?

Mary: *(entering from stage left)* Elizabeth. What are you doing? *(yanks the sack away)*

Elizabeth: I was at the market. I bought you some fresh vegetables for dinner.

Mary: I could have gotten them. You're not supposed to drag heavy things around now.

Elizabeth: I'm not dying, I'm pregnant. I wanted to take a walk.

Mary: But you've got to think of the baby. Especially since, well, since you're kind of old to have one.

Elizabeth: Thank you for stating the obvious. Mary, this baby is a miracle, a gift from God. Now if God wanted me to have this child so badly that he'd let me get pregnant, he's not going to let a few vegetables hurt it.

Mary: *(pulling the chair forward)* Here, sit for a while before going home.

Elizabeth: All right, all right. You're as bad as my husband. I've caught him taking my pulse while I'm sleeping.

Mary: After waiting all these years, I would think you wouldn't want to take any chances.

Elizabeth: I'm not taking chances. I'm very healthy and so is this baby. The only thing that worries me is that with the way he's kicking, he's going to be a handful when he grows up. With my luck, he's going to end up as some wild man who eats locusts.

Mary: Elizabeth, you're my favorite cousin and I love you, but you think really strange thoughts sometimes.

Elizabeth: It comes with my condition ... or maybe my age. Anyway, I have my own dinner to fix. I'll probably see you tomorrow.

Mary: Walk slowly, please. And thanks for the veggies.

(Elizabeth exits stage right. Mary picks up the bowl, moves the sack next to the chair, and sits, beginning to peel carrots. The Angel Gabriel enters from stage left and stands on the platform. He takes a few minutes to prepare himself, signals the audience when he's ready to begin. Mary doesn't notice.)

Gabriel: *(clears throat)* Mary?

(Mary spins completely around, dropping the bowl.)

Mary: Who are you? How did you get in here? My parents will be back any minute. And my father is pretty good with a spear.

Gabriel: *(stepping off platform and walking to Mary)* Calm down. I've been sent from God.

Mary: *(reaching back and grabbing the broom which she wields as a weapon)* God doesn't drop people into kitchens like that. That line might work on Samaritans, but Galileans aren't that naive. Now, get out.

Gabriel: Please listen to me. I'm a messenger. God sent me all the way to earth to tell you something very special.

155

Mary: *(lowering the broom a bit, but still using it as a barrier between herself and Gabriel)* Special message? Why would God have a message for me? I'm not some Pharisee. I don't even know the Torah that well.

Gabriel: Trust me. You have found favor with God. And we never question the Big Guy. Please, if you'd just put down the broom I could explain.

Mary: Okay — you can explain. But please don't walk around too much. I just washed the floor.

Gabriel: Perfectly understandable. May I sit?

Mary: Please do.

(Gabriel sits on the edge of the platform. He takes a moment to regain his composure, pulls out a handkerchief and mops off his forehead. Mary remains standing, leaning on the broom a bit.)

Gabriel: Now as I was saying before I was so rudely interrupted ... Where did you learn to swing a broom like that? You know, one day there's going to be a sport called baseball. Somehow I think you'd be very good at it. Okay *(takes a deep breath and exhales slowly before continuing)*, God has chosen you for a special purpose. You are going to have a baby. This will be a very special child. It will be the Son of God and he will save his people from their sins.

Mary: The Son of God? How can a human have a holy baby? Besides, I'm not even married yet. And, well, I'm not like those girls that hang out by the well.

Gabriel: You are not listening. God will send the baby. He is the one giving you this child, just as he gave the baby to your cousin, Elizabeth.

Mary: That is what Elizabeth was saying before. I'm sorry. None of this makes any sense. I can see you're not of this place, but from God?

Gabriel: I take it you don't know your prophecies that well, either. *(stands and points to the chair)* I can also see you're not going to make this easy for me. I guess you need the demonstration. Sit!

Mary: *(sits on chair)* Okay, but make it quick. That lamb won't cook itself.

Gabriel: I've got other places to go, too, you know. *(clears throat, looks out at audience, this is a presentation he knows by heart)* This story begins many years ago. Prophets like Isaiah and Daniel spoke of a time when God would send a Savior. This Savior would be from the family of David.

Mary: Joseph is from David's family. He talks about it all the time. David was his great, great, great, great, great, great, great....

Gabriel: *(exasperated, cuts her off)* I know that. Anyway, all over the world people have been looking for signs of this Savior. Even in the far-eastern lands.

(Gabriel points to stage left where the first of many visions of the future will be set up. If possible, that end of the stage should have its own lighting. The Kings should set themselves up toward the end of Gabriel's speech about the prophets.)

King 1: *(gazing at the sky)* Where did that star come from? It wasn't in the sky last night.

King 2: I can't find it on any of the charts. And I've gone through all my books.

King 3: A new star that no one has ever seen before. Maybe this is a sign from God. Let's keep an eye on the sky.

King 1: Perhaps the prophecy is finally being fulfilled, and the one we have been waiting for has come.

King 2: The star may lead us to him. I'll tell the servants to begin packing in case we have to leave suddenly.

King 3: I'm going to watch the star a bit longer. I'll let you know if it moves.

King 2: *(mentally making his list)* We'll need several changes of clothing of course, our charts for navigation, food for the animals and ourselves ...

King 3: What about gifts? We can't go visit the Son of God without the right gift.

King 1: We'll bring gold, and frankincense, and costly myrrh. I'll have the servants prepare them at once.

(Kings will exit up center aisle.)

Mary: Who are those guys?

Gabriel: Extremely bright men, some of the most learned on earth. They know the Torah ... and they're not even Jewish.

Mary: Are they looking for this baby I'm supposed to have?

(Mary's Mother enters with bundle, watches scene unfolding before her, then rubs her eyes in disbelief.)

Gabriel: Of course. But that's a little further on in the story. I just wanted to let you know how many people have been waiting for this child. Now, where were we?

Mary: Prophecies.

Mary's Mother: Mary, since when do you let complete strangers in our house?

Mary: Shhh. He's an angel, and he's showing me my future.

Mary's Mother: Like I haven't heard that line before?

Gabriel: Do you mind? I mean, I'm telling a story here. You and Joseph will be married as you've planned. He's going to get cold feet. But don't worry; I'll set him straight. Soon afterward you'll have to go to Bethlehem to pay your taxes. Thank you, Caesar. That's where you'll have the baby.

(As Gabriel speaks, Joseph and a "stand-in" for Mary appear at the back of the auditorium and proceed slowly up the center aisle.)

Mary 2: *(stopping part way)* Please, Joseph. I can't go any further.

Joseph: I know you're tired, Mary. But I've tried every inn in town. There are just no rooms.

Mary 2: There's an inn just ahead. Perhaps they'll have a place for us.

Gabriel: There won't be any rooms at that inn either. But the innkeeper will take pity on you and let you use the stable.

(Mary 2 and Joseph reach platform stage left and settle into the "Christmas Tableau" on platform. The real Mary walks a bit closer to watch.)

Mary's Mother: *(sarcastic)* Oh, wonderful. First, there's an "angel" in my house. Now I find out my daughter is having a baby ... in a stable ... in Bethlehem.

Mary: Hush, Mother. I want to hear this.

Joseph: *(looking over at the real Mary)* The place doesn't matter, Mary. What matters is that you're going to have a healthy boy.

Mary: Joseph, this is all really true? I'm going to have a son?

Joseph: Yes, and we'll call him Jesus. The angel told me that. "His name shall be called Jesus. For he will save his people from their sins."

Mary's Mother: *(turns back to Gabriel, shakes her head as if surprised at what she'd just seen)* I've heard Joseph talk about some of these things. About a child that would come from the line of David and be the Savior of the world. But it's so ...

Gabriel: Weird, strange, bizarre? I know. But, God works in mysterious ways. And, there's more. Shortly after you've had the baby, you'll have visitors.

Mary: *(nodding her head like she knows the answer)* Those wise guys from the East, right?

Mary's Mother: What wise guys?

Mary: I'll tell you later.

Gabriel: No, they won't come 'til much later. It takes a long time to make that journey. No, your visit will be from some shepherds. The star the Wise Men were talking about first appeared to a group of shepherds watching their flocks out in the fields near Bethlehem. It was very late, and most of them were sound asleep. Now, you'll have to excuse me.

(Shepherds enter from stage left and set up their camp in front of where Mary is sitting. Gabriel climbs on to platform.)

Mary: What happens now?

Gabriel: *(puts a finger to his lips)* Just be quiet and watch.

Shepherd 3: *(looks up at sky)* Hey, everybody. Wake up!

Shepherd 2: It's not my turn to watch the sheep yet. Let me sleep.

Shepherd 3: Look at that big star.

Shepherd 2: *(waking up)* Wow, look at it! It's like it's going somewhere. None of the other stars are moving that way. And, it's so bright.

Shepherd 1: *(sitting up)* What star? Where?

Shepherd 3: *(points up and behind)* There. *(as he points, he suddenly notices Gabriel)* Where did you come from?

Gabriel: Fear not, for behold I bring you good tidings of great joy, which shall be to all people.

2nd Angel: For unto you is born this day, in the city of David, a Savior, which is Christ the Lord.

3rd Angel: And this shall be a sign unto you. You shall find the baby wrapped in swaddling clothes and lying in a manger.

Gabriel: *(looking around)* Where's the others?

2nd Angel: Who's missing?

3rd Angel: All the little ones.

2nd Angel: *(to 3rd Angel)* I thought you were bringing them. Can't I trust you with anything?

3rd Angel: *(annoyed and defensive)* Excuse me. Who was walking alongside Mary and Joseph all this way, protecting them? Who had to make sure that innkeeper put people ahead of profits? I've been dealing with an awful lot of stuff here.

2nd Angel: Yeah, but you forgot the first rule of God's kingdom: Children come first!

Gabriel: *(sighing, to 2nd Angel)* Go get the others.

(2nd Angel moves stage right and returns with the little angels.)

Gabriel: Everybody ready?

3rd Angel: We should be. We practiced enough.

2nd Angel: My goodness, we got up on the grumpy side of the clouds this morning. This is important stuff. People are going to be retelling what we do now for thousands of years. Little children are going to say it from church platforms in the twenty-first century! We have to do it right.

3rd Angel: Tell me, were you born high and mighty, or did you have to learn to be that way?

Gabriel: Please, cut it out. You're giving me a headache and there isn't supposed to be any suffering in heaven. *(to the little ones)* Nice and loud, just like we rehearsed it.

All Angels: Glory to God in the highest. Peace on earth, good will toward men.

(Mary mimes applause that Gabriel acknowledges with a slight bow. 3rd Angel also goes to take a bow, but stops when Gabriel gives a stern look. Angels exit stage right.)

Shepherd 2: A Savior? In Bethlehem, of all places. Let's go.

Shepherd 3: But, we want to go, too. And, someone has to watch the sheep.

2nd Angel: I'll do it.

Shepherd 3: Well, I guess that would be okay. Are you sure you can do it?

2nd Angel: No problem.

(Shepherds move from in front of the tableau to behind it.)

Mary: It's so beautiful. To think of all this happening to me.

Gabriel: *(jumping down from the platform next to Mary)* Not just to you, but to all humankind. Well, I've got to go now.

Mary: I'm still not sure I deserve all this.

Gabriel: God has his reasons. What we have to do is just believe in his promises and do what he asks of us.

(Gabriel steps back and walks off the platform. The tableau scene remains a bit longer before lights fade. Then the actors exit left.)

Joseph: *(addressing the real Mary)* Don't be frightened, Mary. It may not be easy at times, but God will give us what we need.

Mary's Mother: I'm going to get your father. Then, you've got a lot of explaining to do, young lady.

(Mary is left alone. As she looks and ponders about what she has seen, another cast member will read Luke 1:46-55. As it is read, Mary will go about straightening up the area, picking up the spilled vegetables, and putting the broom away. Elizabeth enters from stage right, out of breath.)

Elizabeth: Mary, something wonderful has happened. I just know it. I was making my dinner when, all of a sudden, I felt God's presence, and so did the baby. It actually feels like he's dancing in here.

Mary: Oh, Elizabeth, you're right!

Elizabeth: I knew it. God is doing something miraculous.

Mary: For both of us. For all of us. Sit down. I've got a long story to tell you.

Home By Another Way

Characters (in order of appearance)

Narrator	Shepherd 1
Wise Man 1	Shepherd 2
Wise Man 2	Angel
Wise Man 3	Angel Choir
Servant 1	Mary
Servant 2	Joseph
Servant 3	Merchant
Merchant Caravan	Dream Narrator

Props
Campfire
Table
Two chairs
Star
Three gifts
Bundle
Tambourines

Notes

This play uses the journey of the Wise Men to illustrate that God doesn't always call us down the expected path. It also shows the way God often prefers to work through the simplest of people or situations to bring about his plan. It has thirteen speaking parts, plus an "Angel Choir" and "Merchant Caravan" that can incorporate the little ones too small to learn lines.

(Two areas are preset on the stage. One, downstage right, is the campground of the Kings' servants, left behind while the Kings visit King Herod. It requires simply a simulation of a campfire. The second area, stage left, is the home of Mary and Joseph, symbolized by a small table and one or two chairs, with a star hanging above the table.)

Narrator: The Bible says, "God has chosen the foolish to shame the wise." At this time of year, we retell the story of the Wise Men from the East, who followed a star, knowing from ancient prophecy that such a star foretold the coming of the one who would be king and the Messiah. It's a beautiful story, even if people often get it wrong by placing the Wise Men at the manger when the Bible clearly has them coming years later. And, these evidently were extraordinary men of both vision and faith to have undertaken such a long journey merely on the appearance of a star. But, this beautiful picture could have had a horribly ugly ending if these men had listened to the words of a king, instead of the words of an angel ... and maybe, just maybe, the words of the simple shepherds, trades people, and their own servants they met along the way.

We ask you to travel with us this Christmas Eve on the road with the Wise Men and their caravan. We don't claim this is exactly the way it happened but, given that God likes to use the unlikely "tool" to do his work, it could be true.

(Three Wise Men and their caravan of three Servants enter up the center aisle. Servants are carrying the gifts and other bundles. They all stop when they reach the lip of the stage and face forward. The servants group to the left, the Wise Men to the right.)

Wise Man 1: I think we must be getting close. Notice how much slower the star has been moving.

Wise Man 2: Well, that would be true to the prophecies. The prophet Micah says, "But, thou Bethlehem, though thou be little among the thousands of Judah, yet out of these shall he come forth unto me that is to be ruler in Israel." Bethlehem is not very far from here.

Servant 1: *(muttering out loud)* So, why didn't we just go straight there? Honestly, for such smart guys, they make everything so difficult.

Servant 2: Shhh. If you're going to complain about the big guys, at least wait until they can't hear you.

Wise Man 3: Look, there's a palace up ahead. Perhaps the king has already heard news of this child?

Wise Man 2: Yes. We should ask. Any king in this country would surely know the prophecy and would embrace the coming of such a child.

Servant 1: Right. Someone with all the power is really going to welcome the person coming to take his place.

Wise Man 1: *(to Servant 1)* I'm sorry, did you say something?

Servant 1: No, sir. Except, well, it just seems to me that the king might not want to hear about the coming of another king. He might be, I don't know, jealous of him?

Wise Man 2: That is why you are carrying the bags instead of giving the orders. Such a wondrous event as this would overcome any petty feelings like jealousy.

Servant 1: Well, I guess you know best, sir.

Wise Man 2: Yes, I do. So, here's what I think. You find a place to set up camp for the night. Right over there looks fine. We'll go pay our respects to the king and see what he knows. And keep an eye on the sky.

Servant 2: As you wish, sir.

(The Wise Men exit stage left. The Servants move onto the platform stage right and pretend to set up camp.)

Servant 2: Thank goodness for that king. If it hadn't been for that palace, we would have probably walked at least another three miles tonight, and I'm beat. My feet stopped talking to me somewhere around the last olive grove.

Servant 3: So, whose turn is it to cook tonight? I did it last night.

Servant 2: Yeah, and I don't know what hurts worse, my feet or my stomach.

Servant 3: Can I help it if I only know how to cook couscous? I'm used to tending the master's telescopes and sky charts. I never claimed to be a cook. And, I sure never counted on cooking over wood fires in the middle of nowhere.

Narrator: As the servants were preparing the night's meal, a group of shepherds came by with their flock. They were hungry and tired from their long day in the field. So, the servants welcomed them to rest for a while and to share some of their food.

(Shepherds will enter from stage left and join the Servants.)

Shepherd 1: Thank you so much for sharing your dinner. We've had to take the sheep further and further out these days to find grass, so we haven't been home for quite some time.

Shepherd 2: And it's nice to have someone to talk to ... besides the sheep.

Servant 1: Tell me, what do you know about this King Herod?

Shepherd 1: Can we talk about something else? He's a mean old thing.

Shepherd 2: All he cares about is himself and holding on to his power. He does whatever the Romans want so they'll support him.

Servant 1: I knew it. I knew they shouldn't go there.

Servant 3: *(to the Shepherds)* Our masters went to see him to ask about some new king. We've been following that star *(points up)* because it is supposed to mean a king has been born that will be ... what's the word?

Servant 2: A savor.

Servant 1: No, Savior. Someone that will save the people from their sins, and bring about a new world of peace and justice.

Shepherd 1: You talk pretty good for a servant.

Servant 1: That's because I listen to everything the masters say. And, I've read their scrolls.

Servant 2: I'm telling.

Servant 1: And I'm cooking couscous tomorrow.

Servant 2: Okay, I'm not telling.

Shepherd 1: Herod can't tell them anything. He wants to pretend like it didn't happen.

Servant 3: What didn't happen?

Shepherd 2: The birth of the baby. We saw the whole thing.

(As the Narrator speaks the following lines, Angels will enter from stage right and will take the space stage center. The Shepherds will pantomime some of the actions as the Narrator speaks.)

Narrator: And the shepherds then told a wonderful story that happened about a year ago. While they were in the fields, an angel had appeared and they had been very afraid. But the angel told them:

Angel: Fear not. For behold I bring you good news of great joy that shall be to all people. For unto you is born this day, in the city of David, a Savior, which is Christ the Lord. And this shall be a sign unto you. You will find the baby wrapped in swaddling clothes, and lying in a manger.

Narrator: Then the sky was filled with angels, singing praise to God, and saying:

Angel Choir: Glory to God in the highest. Peace on Earth. Good will to men.

Shepherd 1: Then the angels left and we ran to see the baby.

Shepherd 2: They were in a barn behind an inn. The poor little thing was laying in the feedbox, right next to the cows. But, you could tell it was a special baby.

Servant 1: This must be the one our masters are seeking. It's just as the prophecies stated. Tell me, where is the child now?

Shepherd 1: I don't know. They weren't from around here.

Shepherd 2: I heard they went back to Galilee. They were only here to pay their taxes. Thank you, Herod.

Servant 2: Speaking of Herod, the masters will probably be back soon. They may not like us having company.

Shepherd 2: We'll go now. Thanks again for your hospitality.

(Shepherds exit stage right. As they do, the three Wise Men enter from stage left and cross to the campfire.)

Wise Man 1: So, have you kept an eye on the star?

Servant 3: Yes, sirs. It hasn't moved.

Servant 1: But, we met these shepherds. And, sirs, they've seen the baby. It was born in Bethlehem, just like the prophets said ... I mean, you said. And, now, they think it's in Galilee.

Wise Man 2: Shepherds? You'd honestly believe anything a shepherd said?

Wise Man 3: I don't know. Herod obviously knew nothing. He even asked us to report to him what we found.

Wise Man 1: Oh, he was a charming man. And, his palace was beautiful. He invited us to spend the night there on our way back.

Servant 1: Begging your pardon, sir, but I don't think that's a good idea. The shepherds seemed to think Herod was a cruel man, worried about keeping his power. We might be putting the child at risk if you go back.

Wise Man 2: I have had enough of your lip. If we weren't so short-handed, I'd leave you behind. It's not your job to decide what we should and shouldn't do.

Servant 1: I'm very sorry, sir. I'll tend to the camels.

Narrator: After resting that night, the caravan continued for several more days, following the star, which, as the shepherds had said, eventually came to rest over a small house in Galilee. Inside the house, they found the young Jesus, along with his parents, Mary and Joseph.

(During the narration, Mary and Joseph enter stage left and set up their "home" on that part of the stage. Servants pick up the "camp" and, trailing behind the Wise Men, march around the back of the sanctuary, finally coming up the left aisle to Mary and Joseph's home.)

Wise Man 1: Please, is this the home of the one called Jesus?

Wise Man 2: We have traveled so far, following his star. It has finally stopped here. Please tell us our journey has ended.

171

Mary: Yes, the child is here, please come in and let us make you comfortable.

Wise Man 3: We have gifts. Special gifts for a king. Myrrh.

Wise Man 2: Gold.

Wise Man 1: Frankincense.

Joseph: These are very costly gifts.

Mary: But, he is a very special child.

Wise Man 2: We were looking for him in Bethlehem, but the star kept moving here.

Mary: Well, he was born in Bethlehem.

Joseph: To fulfill the prophecies.

Mary: But we're not from there. We only went there to pay our taxes. I'm sorry, this is very overwhelming. Most of those who have come to greet the child have been simple shepherds, some wandering merchants, an innkeeper. No one of your rank or importance.

Wise Man 2: I'm sure we won't be the last. If this is the child whose coming was foretold, why the Emperor himself will want to greet him. And, Herod asked us to tell him where the child was. I know he will be coming. He said so himself.

Joseph: Imagine that? Israel's king coming to see us.

Mary: I don't know, Joseph. He must have heard the stories. If he wanted to come, he would have showed up by now.

Joseph: But, surely, when he hears about it from people like this, he can't help but believe. Before, like you said, it was mostly shepherds. And, you know what people say about shepherds. *(to Wise Men)* Thank you for your gifts. And go and tell Herod what you have seen. But, before you go, may we offer you a meal, something to drink?

Wise Man 1: Thank you, no. We need to make camp before it gets too dark. And, besides, its couscous night. I love couscous cooked over a wood fire.

(Mary and Joseph exit stage left. Caravan exits down center aisle and works its way back up left aisle as the Narrator speaks. They'll eventually set up camp once again on stage right.)

Narrator: The Wise Men and their caravan left the home of Mary and Joseph with all the excitement of a dream fulfilled. The prophecy had come true, and they had lived to see it. They were headed back to their homeland by way of Herod's palace, where they were prepared to tell him all they had seen. The servants were troubled about this, but they knew it would do them no good to tell the Wise Men not to go. They wouldn't listen to them, anymore than Herod would have listened to the Shepherds.

Wise Man 2: Set up camp quickly, servants. I want to go to sleep early so we can be sure of reaching Herod tomorrow.

Wise Man 1: It will be nice to have one night's sleep in a bed at the palace before the long trip home.

Wise Man 3: I've been thinking a lot about this. Maybe, our servants are right and we shouldn't go see Herod.

Wise Man 2: Don't tell me you're starting to believe these wild shepherd stories? We must tell Herod. He's the ruler of this land and it's his right to know.

Wise Man 3: I'm sure you're right.

(A second "caravan," made up of a Merchant and all the little Angels [without costumes], comes up the center aisle, playing tambourines and singing.)

Wise Man 1: Who are those people?

Servant 2: I'm sure it's just some local merchants on their way back from Jerusalem.

Servant 1: Merchants always carry news with them from other villages. It might be a good idea to invite them to join us for dinner.

Wise Man 1: You mean share the couscous?

Servant 2: They can have mine. I was thinking I needed to lose a little weight anyway.

Wise Man 2: Haven't we dealt with enough lowlifes on this trip?

Wise Man 3: No. Invite them. I'd like to hear what's going on.

(All gesture to the caravan to join them.)

Merchant: Thank you for asking us to stop. We haven't had a good hot dinner in several days.

Servant 2: He still won't.

Servant 3: Be quiet. There's nothing wrong with my couscous.

Wise Man 3: So, tell us. What's the news from the outside world? We've been on the road so long; it's been hard to stay in touch.

Merchant: Well, the biggest news I've heard is that Herod is tearing his hair out about some tot. He's called in every mystic, soothsayer, and would-be prophet asking about this child, born a year or so ago, that's supposed to be king. He's even stopping merchants like myself. What am I supposed to know? I'm a date salesman.

Wise Man 2: That's all right. We're headed there tomorrow, and we have the answers he's looking for. You shouldn't be bothered on your return trip.

Merchant: Oh, it's not a bother. It was kind of interesting getting to see the inside of the palace. I mean, Herod would never bother speaking to me before. So, you know the child he's seeking. Do you know him well?

Wise Man 1: We only visited with him once. Why do you ask?

Merchant: Like I said, I'm just a date salesman. But, he had a kind of wild look in his eye. It made me nervous about my own children. Like he might not want to just shake this little one's hand, you know. I think we should get going now. Thanks for the couscous.

Servant 1: By the way, have you seen the child?

Merchant: *(smiling)* I was in Bethlehem to pay my taxes, too. Yes, I've seen the child. And, no, I wouldn't have told Herod even if I did know where he and his family are now.

(Merchant and the caravan exit down center aisle.)

Wise Man 2: I know what you're all thinking. But, I'm not going to take the word of a traveling salesman or a shepherd over a king. It's our duty to report back to Herod. If this child is truly the one, no one can harm him. God wouldn't allow it.

Servant 1: And, maybe the way he wouldn't allow it is by using shepherds and merchants to warn danger away.

Wise Man 2: That's it! I won't have you questioning me again. Leave this camp now.

Wise Man 3: You can't send her away alone in the dark. After we reach the city, you can release her. Now, I suggest we all go to sleep. It's still a day's walk to the castle.

(All pretend to lay down.)

Narrator: While they were sleeping God made sure all three of the Wise Men had a very troubling dream. The dream foretold the evil lurking in Herod's heart.

Dream Narrator: *(offstage, sounding very much like Mr. T from the* A Team*)* Yo, fool! I tried to tell you every other way, but you wouldn't listen. No, you're too good to listen to shepherds and salesmen and servants. So, maybe you'll listen to this. Herod don't want this baby because Jesus is about everything he hates ... justice, peace, a way of life following the teachings of God, not the whims of a power mad fool. Now when you wake up tomorrow, you're gonna take the southern route. It's a lot prettier and there's no Herods. Got it, fool?

Narrator: The three Wise Men woke up suddenly, shaking from the vision.

Wise Man 1: That's it. I'm laying off the couscous for a while.

Wise Man 2: It wasn't the couscous. It was my stubbornness and stupidity. *(calls to Servant 1)* Please bring the maps. I want to avoid even passing near Herod's castle.

Servant 1: *(handing over the maps)* So, we're not going to Herod?

Wise Man 2: I'm a little slow sometimes. I owe you an apology. You were being a good servant, not only to us, but also to the God we were here to honor and obey. I've heard the southern route is very pretty this time of year.

Narrator: And, so the Bible notes, they went home by another way. Sometimes God wants us to seek the long way home; maybe because there's someone along the way we are supposed to help. And, he's not always going to send a dramatic dream to show us the way. So, as we walk or drive our way home, this Christmas Eve, and into the New Year that's about to dawn, stop and listen to the shepherds and salesmen in your lives ... maybe even your own children. And, if needed, be prepared to go home by another way.